W9-DES-087

# COLLECTING MOD

## DESIGN AT THE PHILADELPHIA

# FOREWORD

One of the keys to understanding the development of the collection of the Philadelphia Museum of Art—or, indeed, the history of this institution, especially during the late nineteenth and early twentieth centuries— is the term "industrial art." No longer generally in use, it was once part of the Museum's original title, the Pennsylvania Museum and School of Industrial Art, and clearly expressed the educational goals of its founders and, more specifically, their interest in having the collection serve the useful function of improving the quality of goods designed and manufactured in Philadelphia.

Accordingly, the efforts of the staff of the Museum in the first several decades after its founding in 1876 were directed toward this purpose. In this regard, it is important to note that this endeavor, then as now, encompassed the acquisition not only of significant examples of furniture, ceramics, metalwork, and glass from different historical periods, but also the work of leading designers and manufacturers of the day. This pattern of collecting was purposeful, for it represented the belief that a broad knowledge of the past, of intellectual and artistic traditions, is an essential ingredient of innovation and creativity.

If the author of this study, Kathryn Bloom Hiesinger, the Museum's Curator of European Decorative Arts after 1700, speaks—quite rightly—about the "uneven history" of our collection of decorative arts and design, this should be understood largely as the product, first, of a shift in the educational mission of the Museum, which gradually moved in a direction that no longer directly supported instruction in the disciplines taught at the School of Industrial Art (which eventually separated from the Museum and has since evolved into what is now the University of the Arts) and, second, of the extraordinary changes that occurred in the decorative, or applied, arts during the past century.

If, in retrospect, it is evident that we seemed to have been indifferent to some of those changes or, by contrast, enthusiastic about others, this is not simply a function of the varied judgments of curators and directors that make the shape of any collection like ours distinctive and, at times, even idiosyncratic, but also because of the differing values assigned over time to the acquisition of contemporary work and its relevance to the educational function of this institution. In coming to any judgments about the scope and

Lori Weitzner : for Weitzner Ltd : *Newsworthy* Wallpaper : 2009 : newspaper, nylon : W 47" : 2010-170-1 (cat. 210)

nature of the Museum's collecting efforts in this field throughout its long and distinguished history, the reader should also be mindful of the fact, as Dr. Hiesinger's thoughtful account makes clear, that few fields have changed as dramatically—stylistically, functionally, and technically—as the decorative arts and design have during the period covered by this study.

The publication of *Collecting Modern* would not have been possible without the encouragement and generous financial support of Lisa S. Roberts, who has served on our board of trustees and as a member of Collab, a collaboration of design professionals who support the modern and contemporary design collections at the Philadelphia Museum of Art. The realization of this work, which provides valuable new perspectives on a central and hitherto underappreciated part of our collection, would not have been possible without her assistance, for which we are deeply grateful.

Many members of our staff made essential contributions to the production of this book. Special thanks are due to Graydon Wood and his colleagues in our Photography Department; Sherry Babbitt, The William T. Ranney Director of Publishing; C. Danial Elliott, Arcadia Director of the Library and Archives; and Susan K. Anderson, The Martha Hamilton Morris Archivist, for their support of Dr. Hiesinger throughout the project. Mary Cason skillfully edited the book, which owes its dynamic design to Lisa Benn.

Finally, and most notably, I would like to express our deepest gratitude to Dr. Hiesinger herself, who devoted several years of study to this topic and, it should not go unremarked, has played a prominent role in the development of the Museum's holdings of the decorative arts and design. No one was better qualified to write *Collecting Modern* or could have written a more comprehensive or more sympathetic account of this important chapter in our institutional history.

Timothy Rub

The George D. Widener Director and Chief Executive Officer

Fernando Campana and Humberto Campana : for Alessi : *Peneira* Baskets (3) : 2010 : stainless-steel mesh, natural fiber : D (largest) 15 3/4" : 2010-204-1a–c (cat. 26)

# ACKNOWLEDGMENTS

Having enjoyed the singular experience of developing a modern and contemporary design collection for the Philadelphia Museum of Art over my forty-year curatorial career, I am doubly grateful to Lisa S. Roberts for commissioning this book—which has allowed me the pleasure of recording the achievements of my predecessors and reliving my own. For support in building the collections and programs around them, I am more indebted to members of Collab past and present than I can say. The fact that ninety-five percent of the Museum's design collections have been acquired since the founding of Collab in 1970 bears eloquent witness to the perseverance and generosity of this group of architects, designers, and enthusiasts. No book with a concentrated focus on the history of this Museum—seen through the lens of its contemporary decorative arts collections—could be written without access to the Museum's Archives. I owe a great debt to Susan Anderson, Martha Hamilton Morris Archivist, who shared my joy when I made discoveries and provided information and assistance when I needed help, as well as to her most able colleague, Bertha Adams, project archivist. I would like to extend my enduring gratitude to the Museum's library staff who supplied me with countless books and journal articles to advance and illustrate this study: C. Danial Elliott, Arcadia Director of the Library and Archives; Linda Martin-Schaff, library cataloguer; Ryan McNally, library and visual resources assistant; Rick Sieber, assistant reader services librarian; Evan Towle, librarian for reader services; and Mary Wassermann, librarian for collection development. The Museum's photography department made a special campaign to illustrate this book. For his fine work I am especially grateful to Graydon Wood, senior photographer, as well as to photographers Lynn Rosenthal and James Jason Wierzbicki and to Conna Clark, director of rights and reproductions. My curatorial colleagues answered many questions, particularly among them Dilys Blum, The Jack M. and Annette Y. Friedland Senior Curator of Costume and Textiles. Evan H. Turner and James N. Kise kindly read the text and offered valuable suggestions. For his assistance and patience in preparing the manuscript and assembling the illustrations, I would like to express my heartfelt thanks to Joseph McDermott as well as to Rebecca Chewning, who succeeded him. Finally, it is a pleasure to record my gratitude to Sherry Babbitt, the Museum's William T. Ranney Director of Publishing, for her unfailing interest in and enthusiasm for this project; to Mary Cason, associate editor, who perceptively and vigilantly wrestled the text, notes, and illustrations into intelligible proportions; and to Lisa Benn, whose skills as a designer this book so handsomely demonstrates.

Hella Jongerius : for Porzellan Manufaktur Nymphenburg : *Summer* Teapot from *Four Seasons* : 2007 : glazed hard-paste porcelain, silk : H 10 1/2" : 2010-60-1a–d (cat. 96)

# 1876-
# 1915

# THE MUSEUM'S ORIGINS
# IN A NUCLEUS OF WORKS

The uneven history of the Philadelphia Museum of Art's collections of modern and contemporary decorative arts—known from the later twentieth century as "design"—is the subject of this book. The account rises and falls with the vision and economic fortunes of the institution, its staff, private individuals, and the taste generally for modernism in Philadelphia, which was described by *Good Furniture Magazine* in 1923 as "a big, conservative . . . community that reacts more slowly to innovations than any other city in the country."[1] Over two decades later, in 1944, the Museum's director, Fiske Kimball, reviewed the institution's history of collecting as well as its policies for acquisitions: "It is only fair to say today that prior to 1915, and even down to 1925, the collections of the Museum and of the City, housed at Memorial Hall . . . were—judged by present standards—most inadequate. They comprised . . . the very extensive systematic collections of industrial art assembled by the Museum since 1876 on the model of those at the Victoria and Albert Museum. Valuable for the illustration of types and techniques, they were, with honorable exceptions, lacking in works of high quality." While Kimball noted that the present twentieth-century collections were "very strong," he made an exception for the decorative arts, which were "almost totally lacking."[2] Today, however, the Museum's distinguished collections of modern and contemporary design are among the largest and most important of any comprehensive museum. This is a history with a happy outcome in the present.

The Philadelphia Museum of Art had its origins in the Pennsylvania Museum and School of Industrial Art, which was founded in 1875 on the eve of the Philadelphia International (Centennial) Exhibition of 1876, and given its first home in Memorial Hall (fig. 2), the fine arts exhibition building (the name of the institution would only formally change in 1938; see page 106). In order to form "a nucleus of works of industrial art . . . which, in time, could not fail to have a most beneficial influence upon the industries of our State and City,"[3] a selection committee was appointed by the Museum's newly elected board of trustees to spend $25,000 at the exhibition on the institution's first acquisitions. The committee was headed by William Platt Pepper, vice president of the corporation and managing director of the Museum. Along with Pepper the selection committee consisted of trustees in their capacity as members of four standing committees—on the mechanic arts, materials used in the art industries, the art library, and ornamental art. The latter committee was given overall responsibility for collections, having "entire charge of the purchase and arrangement of works of art as applied to Industry that may be acquired by the corporation."[4] Representing ornamental art on the selection committee were its chair, William Platt Pepper, and Henry C. Gibson; the committee on the art library was represented by its chair, Samuel Wagner, Jr., and Fairman Rogers; and the committees on the mechanic arts and materials used in the art industries, by Thomas Dolan.

The tastemakers on the Museum's board included Philadelphia's educated professional elite as well as self-made men, among them lawyers, physicians, bankers, university professors, civil servants, manufacturers, and art teachers. Some had inherited wealth and social status, others had made their own professional marks and fortunes. William Platt Pepper was a lawyer from a prominent, wealthy Philadelphia family that also included selection committee member Dr. William Pepper, chair and professor of clinical medicine at the University of Pennsylvania (he also served as medical director of the

KUNSTHALLE.    GALERIA DE BELLAS ARTES.    PALAIS DES BEAUX ARTS.

ART GALLERY

Above, top to bottom : **1. Thompson Westcott** : *Centennial Portfolio: A Souvenir of the International Exhibition at Philadelphia* (Philadelphia: T. Hunter, 1876) (cat. 212)   **2.** Art Gallery, Memorial Hall (later Pennsylvania Museum and School of Industrial Art) : 1876 : from *Centennial Portfolio*
Opposite : **3. Artist/maker unknown** (United States) : *Centennial* Handkerchief : 1876 : printed cotton : W 24¼" : 1913-223 (cat. 14)

E PLURIBUS UNUM

MAIN EXHIBITION BUILDING

CENTENNIAL INTERNATIONAL

THE MACHINERY HALL.

MEMORIAL HALL
ART GALLERY

EXHIBITION
FAIRMOUNT PARK
PHILADELPHIA
1776    1876

THE AGRICULTURAL HALL.

THE HORTICULTURAL HALL.

Centennial Exhibition). Unlike the Peppers, Dolan was born "of obscure ancestry"[5] but made his fortune manufacturing textiles and clothing during the Civil War. Gibson was a prosperous real estate developer who inherited money from his father's whiskey-distilling company. Wagner was a lawyer and bibliophile, and Rogers was a civil engineer and professor of civil engineering at the University of Pennsylvania (which he represented on the Museum's board). Rounding out the selection committee were Coleman Sellers and John Baird. Sellers, president of the board of trustees, was a well-known engineer and inventor who also had served from 1870 to 1875 as president of Philadelphia's Franklin Institute, founded for the promotion of the mechanic arts in 1824. His maternal grandfather was the American painter Charles Willson Peale (1741–1827), a pedigree that gave him considerable clout among the art-minded in Philadelphia. Baird was a marble supplier (for the extension of the Capitol in Washington, D.C., among other projects) and chaired the Museum's building committee.

Connected by wealth and civic interest, the selection committee combined members who were considered to have good aesthetic judgment—notably Gibson, Sellers, and William Platt Pepper—with

those appointed for their ability to apply an interest in science and technology to art, thereby fusing industry and artistic concerns. As the Museum's didactic mission was intended to demonstrate the inseparability of art and science, the initial program for collecting was not confined to works of art, but also extended to patented inventions as well as plant and animal materials. Among the aesthetes, judged by their later gifts to the Museum, William Platt Pepper seemed personally interested in archaeological and non-Western objects, ranging from Pre-Columbian pottery (given in 1883) to Persian ceramics (1891) to Chinese bamboo screens (1894). Gibson, partnering with fellow trustees Francis W. Lewis and Clarence H. Clark, gave the Museum an eighteenth-century Chinese wall hanging in 1885 and a handsome group of transfer-printed English earthen-ware in 1889. When Pepper resigned as the Museum's managing director in 1879, the board urged him to continue as vice president (he did), so that the Museum "could continue to enjoy the benefit of his cultivated taste and excellent judgement in those depart-ments of industry and art in which this Institution is particularly interested."[6]

The *Philadelphia Times* reported in the fall of 1876 the selection committee's purchases of both historic and contem-porary objects.[7] The latter embraced the fashionable historicizing styles exemplified by Thomas John Bott, Jr.'s porcelain ewer (fig. 4) and stand designed for the Worcester Royal Porcelain Company in imitation of sixteenth-century Limoges copper-ground enamels—an impressive technical feat noted by contemporaries. Bott's ewer and stand were one of thirteen pieces of porcelain

4. Thomas John Bott, Jr. : for Worcester Royal Porcelain : Ewer : 1875 : enameled and gilt porcelain : H 11¼" : 1876-1623 (cat. 23)

and earthenware purchased at the Centennial Exhibition for $1,600 from the stand of the London china merchant A. B. Daniell and Son (fig. 6), which represented two firms, Minton and Worcester. The Minton display included parian porcelains with *pâte-sur-pâte* and gilt decoration in the "Greek" style by Marc-Louis-Emmanuel Solon; from this display the Museum purchased two vases, *L'Échange* and *La Grace* (fig. 5)—the first of several pieces by Solon that the Museum would acquire. The selection committee described these works as "remarkable for their excellence of workmanship and artistic design."[8] The committee also bought thirty-three examples of pottery and tiles from the British firm of Doulton & Company for a total of $550,[9] including an oval platter painted by Mary Butterton with a Persian-style design of scattered foliage (fig. 11). The platter perhaps appears more modern to us today than do other pieces from the exhibition because of the decoration's loose arrangement on a plain ground and reliance on a non-Western source. Gifts from manufacturers added to the Museum's initial collection, including a cut-glass wine set made by the Dorflinger Glass Company of White Mills, Pennsylvania, the decanter bearing among other decorations the seal of the city of Philadelphia and the name of its mayor in 1876 (fig. 7). Japanese potter Riokei Nakashima gave the Museum a pair of porcelain jars from his manufactory at

Satsuma "in grateful memory [of] the Eminent services rendered to my country by your great Naval Commander Commodore Perry, and the kindness which the Japanese have at all times received from your citizens."[10] The selection committee added an earthenware tray also made (and decorated) by Nakashima, and purchased directly from him (fig. 57).

In retrospect, the committee seems to have overlooked several displays that we would consider important today, among them, that of Vienna's pioneering bentwood furniture firm of Gebrüder Thonet. However, nearly a century later the Museum was able to purchase a collection of twelve bentwood chairs made after the designs of Michael Thonet and his successors (figs. 9, 10). Although wallpapers made by Morris and Company were given to the Museum in 1876 by an anonymous donor, many decades would pass before other examples of British Arts and Crafts would enter the collections, including a marquetry cabinet designed by George Washington Jack for Morris and Company (fig. 12) and a high-back chair designed by Charles Rennie Mackintosh about 1897 for the Argyle Street Tea Rooms in Glasgow (fig. 56). Souvenirs of the exhibition were also acquired in later years, such as Thompson Westcott's handsomely illustrated *Centennial Portfolio* (fig. 1) and a cotton handkerchief printed with views of the Centennial buildings (fig. 3), the latter given by Mrs. William D. Frishmuth, a noted collector of musical instruments and early American decorative arts.[11]

5. **Marc-Louis-Emmanuel Solon** : for Minton : *La Grace* Vase : 1875 : glazed and gilt Parian porcelain : H 15 3/16" : 1876-1620,a (cat. 178)

6. A. B. Daniell and Son at the Centennial Exhibition : 1876

7. Dorflinger Glass Company · Decanter and Wineglasses · 1876 · glass · H (decanter) 16¼" · H (glass) 5" · 1876.1693, 1693II (cat. 46)

Above : **8. Rörstrand** : Plate : 1876 : glazed earthenware : D 20" : 1897-617 (cat. 162)    Opposite, left to right : **9. Gebrüder Thonet** : Desk Chair, *Model No. 9* : c. 1870 : beechwood, caning : H 29 3/8" : 1969-136-9 (cat. 186)    **10. Gebrüder Thonet** : Chair, *Model No. 51* : c. 1890–1900 : beechwood, caning : H 36 5/8" : 1969-136-8 (cat. 187)

**11. Mary Butterton** : for Doulton : Dish : c. 1876 : glazed earthenware : W 7⁷/₁₆" : 1876-64 (cat. 25)

12. George Washington Jack : for Morris and Company : Secretaire Cabinet : c. 1889 : mahogany, hardwoods : H 51½" : 1986-128-1a,b (cat. 87)

# SETTING AN EXAMPLE FOR
# INDUSTRY AND THE PUBLIC

The character of the institution that the selection committee hoped to form had been defined earlier as "a Museum of Art,"[12] and once, in passing, as a "Museum of Industrial, Decorative and Antiquarian Art."[13] Following a report "on Museums of Art in Europe and in this country" made by the provisional committee that drafted the Museum's charter in 1875, the fledgling institution was created as the Pennsylvania Museum and School of Industrial Art, with a mission "to be in all respects similar to that of the South Kensington Museum of London,"[14] which was also associated with an art school known originally as the School of Design. The Pennsylvania Museum would remain linked to its school until 1964, when the latter achieved independent status as the Philadelphia College of Art (later the University of the Arts).[15] Like the collections of the South Kensington (later the Victoria and Albert) Museum, those of the Pennsylvania Museum were intended to instruct and improve by example the taste of industry and its students as well as that of the general public. Such optimistic faith in the natural abilities of all individuals to learn and judge critically shaped committee members' attitudes toward the Museum's uneducated audience, and toward themselves as connoisseurs and arbiters of taste. Pressure to emphasize the institution's pedagogical purpose through its collections came from the state of Pennsylvania. In his 1876 annual address Governor John F. Hartranft, who served (ex-officio) on the Museum's board, pointed out that Pennsylvania lacked "industrial education" to train "intelligent farmers, manufacturers, miners, and mechanics," and that the Centennial Exhibition (fig. 14) had brought the opportunity to establish a museum and school in Memorial Hall wherein "to form an art library; special collections, illustrative of industrial processes[;] and a thorough system of instruction in the arts of design as applied to manufactures, accompanied by general and technical lectures." The institution would contain, according to Hartranft, "the nucleus of a collection . . . intended to promote the improvement of American industrial art."[16] Accordingly, along with the fine contemporary English ceramics described above, the selection committee purchased and acquired by gift a wide range of objects and materials in the fields of art, science, and natural history, including historic and contemporary textiles (figs. 13, 20) and fifty-six specimens of Belgian flax meant to enlighten Philadelphia's economically important textile industry. Whether or not related to collecting textiles, in 1879 the Entomological Section of the Academy of Natural Sciences presented the Museum with a collection of insects.[17]

The committee's first acquisition, described by the *Philadelphia Times* as "the most interesting purchase yet," was from Elkington and Company of London: "their complete collection of electrotype reproductions of the original artistic works in gold, silver, bronze, iron and other metals," which had been collected by and then exhibited at the South Kensington Museum. As the newspaper noted, "Those originals represent the artistic work in metal of all ages and all climes, and all that the student can learn from them he can learn from the reproductions" (figs. 17, 19).[18] In addition, the selection committee also reported to the board that it had purchased for $1,500 from the Centennial's Egyptian exhibit "the collections of casts in plaster and zinc of Arabic ornament taken directly from the mosques and tombs for the first time by order of the Khedive."[19] While today we would argue that the value to the student lies more in the experience of an original, unique work of art than in a reproduction of it, the collecting of reproductions and casts for teaching purposes by museums, schools, and universities had a long history in the nineteenth century. Plaster casts of antiquities in particular were assiduously collected to provide access to great works of art at little cost. Art students in Europe and the United States—

13. Artist/maker unknown (Caucasus) : Pieced Cover : c. 1876 : wool, silk : H 19¾" : 1876-507 (cat. 8)

including the Philadelphia painter Thomas Eakins, who studied at the Pennsylvania Academy of the Fine Arts—routinely drew from casts until they were deemed proficient enough to work from live models. By the end of the century, however, the Pennsylvania Museum, along with other American museums, began to shift away from collecting casts to acquiring original works as the latter became available from private European collections and archaeological digs. Still, as late as 1935 the Museum's board of trustees authorized the school principal to purchase three casts from the "Florentine Art Shop" for $35.00.[20]

Already in the fall of 1876, while waiting for Memorial Hall to be refurbished as a museum, the board of trustees asked the committee on ornamental art to inquire into the possibility of exhibiting the Museum's first acquisitions at the Pennsylvania Academy of the Fine Arts.[21] The exhibition was also to include loans, some borrowed from private collections.[22] Smoothing the way for the request to use the academy's space was John Sartain, a well-respected artist and printmaker, member of the Museum's committee on instruction, and long-serving and influential board member of the academy. Sartain had also headed the fine arts section at the Centennial Exhibition in Memorial Hall. Thus from January to March 1877 the Museum's *Art Applied to Industries* exhibition was shown at the academy, tickets required. The exhibition was not financially successful, although the deficit was said to have been "more than repaid by subscriptions from those whose

14. Opening Day Ceremony at the 1876 Centennial Exhibition : Art Gallery at Memorial Hall

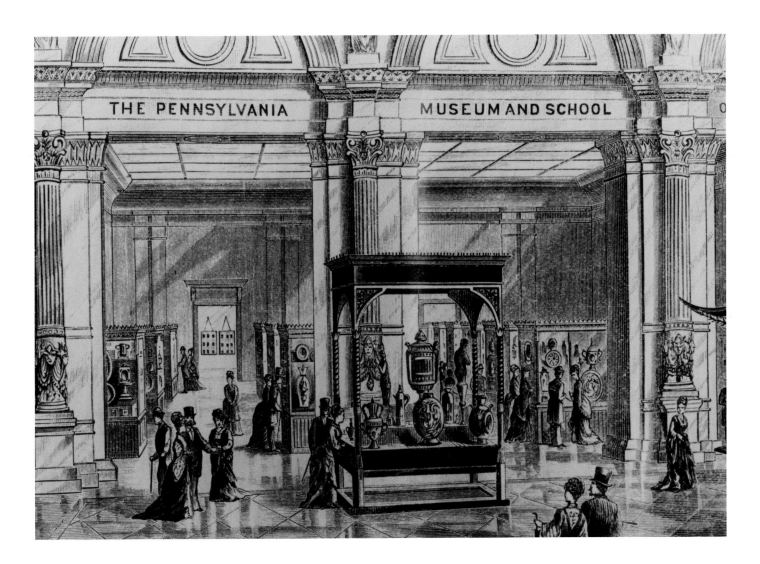

THE PENNSYLVANIA · MUSEUM AND SCHOOL · O

interest was aroused."[23] At the close of the exhibition, the objects were moved to Memorial Hall by direction of the committee on ornamental art, and then displayed to the public on May 10, 1877, at the opening of the Pennsylvania Museum and School of Industrial Art (fig. 15).[24]

Following the example of the South Kensington Museum, the Pennsylvania Museum organized and displayed its collections by medium and technique of manufacture, "grouping together, so far as practicable, objects of similar character, and perfecting the plan of labelling, in order that the visitors might be informed of the exact character of each object, and be enabled to study them more intelligently."[25] Contemporary English and French ceramics and glass were lent to the Museum by A. B. Daniell and

Son as well as Londros & Co., also of London, along with Spanish glass and pottery recommended by the scholar Juan Riaño, who had catalogued the Spanish objects at South Kensington.[26] These loans were all negotiated and arranged, with an option to purchase, by the director of the South Kensington Museum, Philip Cunliffe-Owen, who had himself purchased a group of Persian objects for the Pennsylvania Museum. Faith in Owen, who had advised the Museum since its inception, was both boundless and well founded. Around this time the Museum corporation also allowed the American Institute of Mining Engineers to display its Centennial exhibition of mining and metallurgy in Memorial Hall, arguing that "this material is of the greatest interest and value as bearing upon one of the most important industries of the State, and although not

15. Early rendering of the Pennsylvania Museum and School of Industrial Art : c. 1877

Centennial Photographic Co. Philada.

International Exhibition, 1876.

34

Centennial Photographic Co. Philada.

International Exhibition, 1876.

28

**16–19. Stereographs by Edward L. Wilson** from *The Collection of the Pennsylvania Museum and School of Industrial Art* (Philadelphia: Centennial Photographic Company, c. 1877) : gelatin silver prints    Clockwise from top left : **16. Philippe-Joseph Brocard** : Lamp : glass    **17. Antoine Vechte** : Salver : silvered electrotype reproduction    **18. Charles Toft** : for Minton : Candlestick and Biberon : glazed earthenware    **19. Artist/maker unknown** : *Jamnitzer* Cup :  silvered electrotype reproduction

possessing any art character, is quite in keeping with two of the departments of the original Museum plan, that of the Raw Material collection, and of the collection illustrative of the Mechanic Arts."[27] Although supported strongly by the governor and certain trustees, this was a decision the Museum corporation was soon and long to regret: the material occupied much valuable exhibition space, and the parameters of the Museum's collections would change within a decade.

In early 1878 the trustees decided to send the corporation's secretary, H. Dumont Wagner, to the international exhibition being held in Paris from May to October of that year.[28] He was given $1,500 to spend on "works of art applied to Industry as may in his judgment be suitable."[29] Wagner also served as special commissioner for Pennsylvania to inquire into the systems of industrial art education then current in Europe.[30] However, he could find little at the exhibition to buy for the Museum, judging that "the objects exhibited, the value of which was within the means of the Museum, differed little from those of the same class purchased at the Centennial Exhibition." He consequently "bought but few specimens, considering it best to purchase books on industrial art"[31] for the library, to which was added eventually Jules Goury and Owen Jones's important two-volume publication on the Alhambra (fig. 25), which demonstrated to its readers the potential of non-European—particularly Islamic—decoration. At

£2,000, objects such as Bruce Talbert's prize-winning Anglo-Japanese cabinet for Jackson and Graham might have been beyond the Museum's budget (it was sold to the khedive of Egypt), or considered too close to the Japanese lacquered cabinet purchased at the Centennial from the Imperial Japanese Commission (fig. 24), but countless other, smaller objects could have been purchased, notably ceramics by Émile Gallé, to further develop the handsome, affordable collection in that medium begun in 1876.

It may have been regret for an opportunity lost that spurred the trustees to purchase the following year examples of enameled glass by Philippe-Joseph Brocard, France's first modern artist-glassmaker, as well as glazed earthenware by Joseph-Théodore Deck, the most influential and technically progressive ceramist in France. These adventurous purchases, described as "interesting specimens of Industrial Art,"[32] were acquired from among the loans made by the firm of Londros to the Museum's inaugural exhibition at Memorial Hall. Sadly, none of these works, like the vast number of acquisitions made by the selection committee in 1876, have survived in the Museum's collections—all sold, unlocated, damaged and destroyed, or transferred to other institutions (figs. 16–19). However, since 1969 a number of works by Deck in the exotic non-Western styles he championed have finally reentered the collections (fig. 22).

Opposite : **20. Artist/maker unknown** (Turkey) : Quilt Facing *(Yorgan Yüzü)* (detail): c. 1300–1919 : linen, silk : W 50" : 1877-18 (cat. 13)
Above : **21. Giacinto Melillo** : Pair of Earrings : c. 1870 : gold, enamel, pearl : L 4 3/8" : 1925-27-337a,b (cat. 127)

22. Joseph-Théodore Deck : Dish : 1863 : glazed and enameled earthenware : D 18¹³/₁₆" : 1978-117-1 (cat. 44)

23. W. T. Copeland & Sons : Pitcher : c. 1876 : glazed earthenware : H 10½" : 1897-522 (cat. 37)

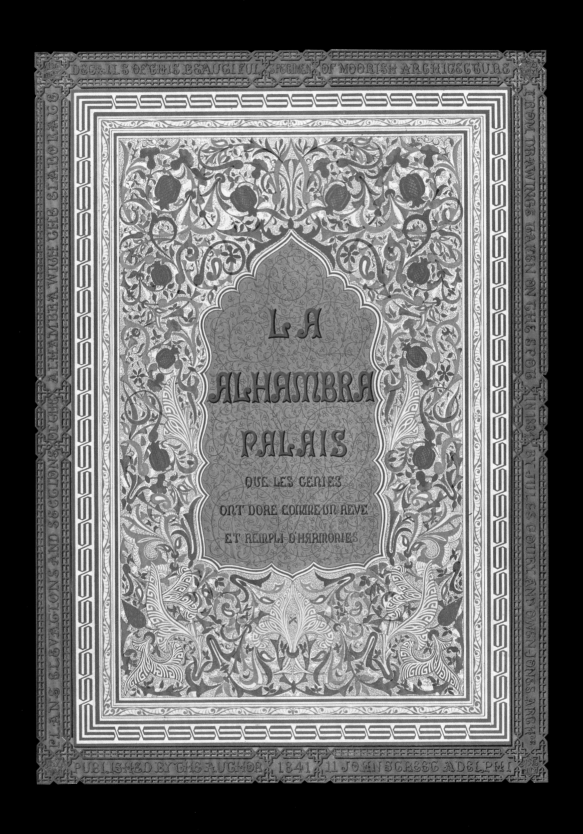

Opposite : **24. Artist/maker unknown** (Japan) : Cabinet : c. 1876 : lacquered wood, horn, mother-of-pearl, jade, bronze, malachite : H 5' 4¹/₂" : 1876-1681 (cat. 12)   Above : **25. Jules Goury and Owen Jones** : *Plans, Elevations, Sections, and Details of the Alhambra* (London: Owen Jones, 1842–45) : title page of vol. 1 (cat. 74)

The board recommended in November 1892 that funds be raised for the purpose of purchasing objects the following year at the World's Columbian Exposition in Chicago.[64] Mrs. William Weightman and John T. Morris both advanced the Museum funds to send Dorr and school principal Leslie Miller to Chicago.[65] Dorr, Morris, and Barber went separately to the exposition on behalf of the Museum, and each purchased contemporary ceramics—particularly American art pottery—for the collection. In October 1893 Morris wrote Dorr from Chicago: "How much, *how much* could be done here with $5,000. Think over the propriety of making an appeal in the papers making clear to the people the advantages which can be derived from a little ready cash."[66] Pepper urged Dorr to visit the exposition: "Your trip to Chicago would be of advantage to the Museum and as you have had letters from Exhibitors offering gifts—you would be able to tell whether the proposed gifts are worth accepting for we don't want a lot of trash shunted off on us."[67] When Dorr arrived in Chicago, Barber advised him of his own negotiations with various exhibitors: "I sent you yesterday through the Museum a letter from the Lonhuda pottery of Steubenville, Ohio, in which they offered us some good specimens of their ware. I hope you will see that it is secured before you leave Chicago and packed for shipment."[68] Other manufacturers were equally generous, among them the Ohio Valley China Company of Wheeling, West Virginia, which gave the Museum a spectacular neo-rococo porcelain centerpiece (fig. 35), and the Edwin Bennett Pottery Company of Baltimore, which donated "Numerous Specimens of their Manufacture,"[69] including a Persian-style pitcher with painted and gilt arabesque decoration (fig. 32). Founded only several years earlier, in 1880, by Maria Longworth of Cincinnati, the innovative Rookwood Pottery was a great favorite of Dorr, Morris, and Barber. The collection of "historic" American pottery and porcelain assembled by Barber and sold to the Museum on his appointment as curator included early Rookwood, as well as examples of other American art pottery. In addition, William Watts Taylor, president of Rookwood, presented the Museum with fifteen pieces, of which only one survives today in the Museum's collections (fig. 31).[70]

Opposite : **31. Albert Robert Valentien** : for Rookwood : Vase : 1886 : glazed stoneware : H 11 1/2" : 1976-45-1 (cat. 197)    Above : **32. Edwin Bennett Pottery Company** : Pitcher : 1893 : glazed and gilt earthenware : H 12 1/2" : 1893-368 (cat. 18)

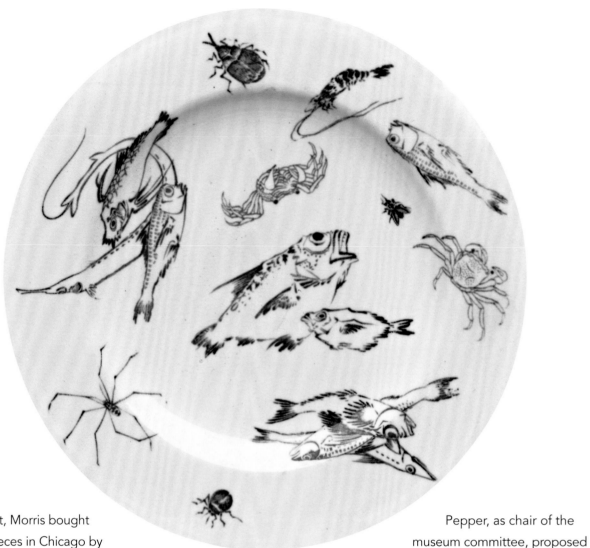

As was his wont, Morris bought a number of pieces in Chicago by different artists and manufacturers, which he or his sister Lydia T. Morris gave either immediately or eventually to the Museum. Among the best and most impressive were a large salt-glazed stoneware jar, lid, and stand with modeled and applied decoration by Susan Frackelton of Milwaukee, Wisconsin (fig. 34), and an important "Greek" vase by Marc-Louis-Emmanuel Solon for Minton. The vase had been made in 1887 and already shown with its pair at the Paris Universal Exposition of 1889. Thoroughgoing, Morris wrote directly to the artist to inquire about its subject. Solon replied: "This time the subject is very simple, and chosen chiefly as an occasion of showing female figures in varied attitudes. It is not to be forgotten that this vase is only one of a pair. On the two vases were contrasted: 'Grace and Strength.'"[71] In 1898

Pepper, as chair of the museum committee, proposed to the board the purchase of another masterwork by Solon, the *Jester* vase, from Bailey, Banks and Biddle of Philadelphia.[72] The purchase price of $1,500 was drawn from the Temple Fund, and again the artist provided a description of his subject: "In the guise of a Court Jester, the frolicsome Nymph confides to her puppet the secret of the many tricks she has just played. From the branches of a tree hang the masks of various expressions she has worn. . . . On the reverse of the vase a puppet-show is seen, in which little wooden actors are giving a performance of 'Minerva, Goddess of Wisdom, Overpowered and Vanquished by Love'" (fig. 58).[73] Pepper, now the Museum's director, wrote Morris about installing the vase and suggested that it deserved "a case of its own—for it is a *most important piece* & worthy of

Opposite : **33. Rookwood Pottery** : Plate : 1880 : glazed stoneware : D 8¾" : 1976-104-1 (cat. 161)    Above : **34. Susan Frackelton** : Jar on Stand : 1893 : glazed stoneware : H 25" : 1893-309,a,b (cat. 59)

being alone and being made much of. I suppose there is no better specimen in America than that—certainly not in any Museum and it cost a lot of money."[74]

Barber was a serious scholar of ceramics history and technology, writing books, catalogues, and articles that not only did credit to his reputation and that of the Museum, but also made the institution's growing collections—then largely acquired by Barber himself—widely known for the first time in the United States and abroad. In the January 1892 issue of *Popular Science Monthly*, Barber published "Recent Advances in the Pottery Industry," which described the rise of American art potteries in Bennington, Vermont; Phoenixville, Pennsylvania; East Liverpool, Ohio; and Cincinnati, home of Rookwood Pottery, "the first in this country to demonstrate the fact that a purely American art-production, in which original and conscientious work is made paramount to commercial considerations, can be appreciated by the American public."[75] Noting that the Japanese ceramics display at the Philadelphia Centennial Exhibition had perhaps more than anything else inspired the establishment of Rookwood,[76] Barber illustrated the point by means of a dish decorated with fish after Japanese prints (fig. 33). This Rookwood piece came to the Museum with the purchase of Barber's collection in 1892 by John T. Morris, who presented another Rookwood Japanese-style piece the following year; it had been purchased either at the Chicago exposition or, as Barber reported to Dorr, at auction in Philadelphia.[77]

Together Morris and Barber developed the Museum's modern as well as historic ceramic collections, the board member often funding the curator's purchases. The correspondence between the two men about works of art, often on a daily basis and lasting until Morris's death in 1915, records the opinions of two passionate collectors as they acquired objects for themselves and the Museum. Barber's authority in the field of American ceramics was definitively established with the publication in 1893 of his

magisterial volume *The Pottery and Porcelain of the United States: An Historical Review of American Ceramic Art from the Earliest Times to the Present Day*, a book that, as he stated in the preface, was the result of "thorough personal investigations . . . study of the products of the potteries in the United States, and . . . consultation with intelligent potters in the leading establishments of the land."[78] As usual, Barber illustrated works from his own collection that had been acquired by the Museum, and in subsequent editions of the book added other Museum pieces.

For the next twenty years Morris and Barber shopped and bought incessantly, visiting potteries, dealers, auction houses, and exhibitions separately and together, submitting their finds to each other for review, agreeing and disagreeing—sometimes strongly but always with great respect. In March 1896 Barber wrote Dorr of his trip to Trenton with Morris: "I brought home a few little pieces as gifts from potters, which I would like to send out to the Museum. . . . Since returning I have written to a couple of the Potteries that we visited, asking for some other small pieces which I happened to see when we were there."[79] Three months later Barber wrote again: "After working for more than a year, I have finally secured some additional examples of recent types of pottery made at the Rookwood Pottery";[80] he later reminded Dorr, "I suppose you have sent an acknowledgment to Mr. W. W. Taylor of Cincinnati, for his recent gift of Rookwood pieces. I had the pleasure of seeing these when I was last out."[81] Taylor's gift included a handsome vase in the *Iris* glaze line, decorated by Constance Amelia Baker in 1896. It was probably during Barber's 1896 trip to Cincinnati that he designed his own tankard for Rookwood, duly stamped with his name and dated 1896. He tended to be an encyclopedic, academic collector, attempting to document each new form or decoration, however slight the variation, as he chronicled the history of American pottery. This was an attitude to which Morris took constant exception, as Barber reported to Dorr with regard to some early nineteenth-century pieces: "I had a talk with Mr. Morris some weeks ago in

35. Carl Goetz : for Ohio Valley China : Centerpiece : 1892 : glazed and unglazed porcelain : H 25 1/2" : 1893-376a (cat. 73)

regard to a similar series, though not so complete as this, but did not press the matter as I saw that he felt that the pieces had no artistic value. This is very true, as some of them are extremely crude, but so far as I am concerned personally, I am far more interested in seeing our collection of historic objects complete than in procuring at the present time modern pieces of artistic ware. I desire to see the collection illustrating the progress and development of the art in this country, as complete and unbroken as possible, and for this reason I trust the Museum can afford to raise the small amount necessary to secure this lot."[82]

The 1890s brought to the Museum two important ceramic collections, primarily historic, although each collection included some modern pieces: that of the Reverend Alfred Duane Pell of New York, beginning in 1894 with a gift of English and European porcelain and continuing until Pell's death in 1924 (Pell was named the Museum's honorary curator of European porcelain in 1904[83]); and that of General Hector Tyndale of Philadelphia, bequeathed to the Museum in 1897 by his widow, Julia N. Tyndale. Coproprietor of a fine-ceramics firm, Tyndale had chaired the jury for pottery at the Centennial Exhibition; his bequest included works by contemporary Japanese potters and a pitcher by W. T. Copeland and Sons in the Japanese style (fig. 23). Despite Barber's success in acquiring objects for the collection, he was unhappy about the appearance of the ceramic gallery at Memorial Hall, complaining to Dorr in 1896: "When I was last out I was very much impressed with the unfavorable conditions

Above, left to right : **36. Louis Comfort Tiffany** : for Tiffany : Vase : 1899 : Favrile glass : H 10³/₄" : 1901-59 (cat. 189)    **37. Louis Comfort Tiffany** : for Tiffany : Vase : c. 1900 : Favrile glass : H 5¹³/₁₆" : 1901-58 (cat. 190)    Opposite : **38. Louis Comfort Tiffany** : for Tiffany : Vase : c. 1900 : Cypriote glass : H 9³/₈" : 1901-63 (cat. 191)

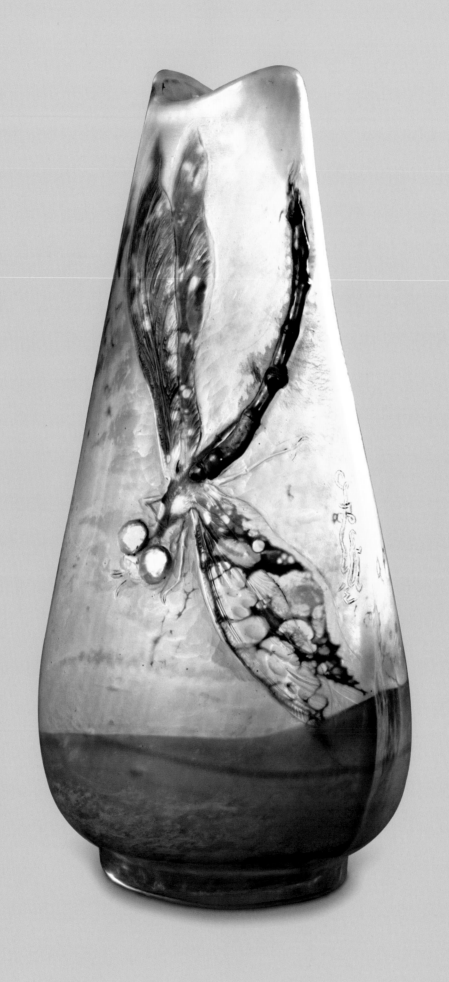

for exhibiting the American collection. The cases are entirely too crowded and the best objects do not show to advantage. The collection also needs rearrangement and I shall be ready at almost any time to arrange it properly when suitable case room has been provided."[84] Nevertheless, in December 1899 he could write to Morris: "On every side I hear nothing but praise for our *American* collection. It is attracting a great deal of interest and several of the papers have called attention to it."[85] This view was seconded by Pepper, who praised the collection as "unequalled by any other Museum."[86]

In 1900, while Barber was working on a revision of his publication *Anglo-American Pottery: Old English China with American Views*,[87] and acquiring the collections to illustrate it, Morris went to Paris to purchase ceramics and

glass at the Universal Exposition, returning with Hungarian art pottery from the Zsolnay factory and porcelains from the Parisian firm of Camille Naudot (fig. 40), the Royal Copenhagen Porcelain Manufactory, the Royal Porcelain Manufactory in Berlin, and the Gustavsberg and Rörstrand factories in Sweden, along with ten boxes of Tiffany glass (figs. 36–38), and French glass by Cristallerie de Pantin and Émile Gallé (figs. 41, 42). Morris must have been particularly fond of the pieces by Naudot, as he asked Barber whether he was going to illustrate any of the new objects from Paris in the Museum's next annual report, pointing particularly to "the little cup with inlaid enamel . . . the newest thing in the porcelain line."[88] Barber was not entirely familiar with some of the European pieces Morris had bought, writing: "In making the labels for the Paris pieces, I find that you purchased one of the pieces (cameo

Opposite : **39. Émile Gallé** : Vase : c. 1903–4 : patinated glass with applied decoration, metal foil : H 11 1/2" : 1905-46 (cat. 63)
Above : **40. Camille Naudot, Fils et Cie.** : Bowl : c. 1900 : enameled soft-paste porcelain : D 4 15/16" : 1901-45 (cat. 134)

glass) from Stumpf, Violett & Cie., 84 Rue de Paris at Pantain [*sic*]. I am not clear as to whether this firm made the glass or simply sold it to you? Kindly give me the name of the maker, if other than the above" (they were the same; fig. 43).[89] Many decades later the Museum was able to add to the collections two additional groups of European porcelain that had also been shown in Paris: a tea set designed by J. Jurriaan Kok and painted by W. P. Hartgring for the Rozenburg factory in The Hague (fig. 45), and two figures from the *Jeu de l'Echarpe* series designed by Agathon Léonard for Sèvres.

With regard to the ten boxes from Tiffany, Pepper had written to Morris, possibly on Barber's recommendation,

requesting that he spend $1,000 of the Temple Fund on a selection of Tiffany Favrile glass at the Paris Exposition.[90] It is likely that Pepper had already seen the glass, as he wrote Dorr: "The Tiffany Favrile Glass people have sent me a notice that the articles they are to send to the Paris Exhibition are now on view at their place in New York. I want to try to get in to see them, if possible toward the close of this week or the middle of next week."[91] Like the works of Solon and the Rookwood Pottery, Tiffany glass was and continued to be a favorite of Morris, Barber, and the board as a whole. Buying in quantity, the Museum became the largest institutional collector of Tiffany glass of the period. While in Paris, Morris also purchased American art pottery, including three Rookwood vases,

Above, left to right : **41. Émile Gallé** : Vase : c. 1900 : glass with marquetry decoration : H 8 1/8" : 1900-219 (cat. 61)     **42. Émile Gallé** : Vase : 1900 : glass with marquetry decoration : H 6 3/16" : 1921-46-71 (cat. 62)     Opposite : **43. Stumpf, Touvier, Viollet & Cie.** : Vase : c. 1900 : glass with wheel-cut decoration : H 8" : 1900-145 (cat. 185)

one of them a masterwork, a large vase decorated with delicately translucent roses on a glossy black ground by the Japanese artist Kataro Shirayamadani (fig. 44); Morris also bought six examples of faience from the Boston firm of Grueby.

Barber, meanwhile, had been occupied with his historic collections of American pottery, proposing numerous acquisitions after Morris's return from Paris. Morris, for once, had tired of Barber's constant solicitations: "I have examined the plates sent me and I am sorry to differ with you regarding the desirability of purchasing. I have spent so much money on the Museum this year, and as it seems impossible to secure the 'last plate' I have decided to let someone else have all but #6 for which I send [a] check."[92] Barber was apparently undaunted, as Morris again wrote him, with exasperation, in late 1901: "I agree with you it would be desirable for us to have the small plate but do you not think you are pushing me a little hard?"[93] Once more, three months later, Morris wrote, "The Museum is constantly on my thoughts but really Mr. Barber, sometimes accumulations occur when I must give some attention to my own business."[94]

Opposite : **44. Kitaro Shirayamadani** : for Rookwood : Vase : 1899 : glazed stoneware : H 17 3/8" : 1901-15 (cat. 176)    Above : **45. J. Juriaan Kok and Wilhelmus Petrus Hartgring** : for Haagsche Plateelbakkerij Rozenburg : Tea Service : 1900 : enameled soft-paste porcelain : H (teapot) 7 1/2" : 1975-18-1–6 (cat. 101)

# BVLLETIN OF THE PENNSYLVANIA MVSEVM

PVBLISHED QVARTERLY
BY THE
**PENNSYLVANIA MVSEVM**
AND
**SCHOOL OF INDVSTRIAL ART**
MEMORIAL HALL
FAIRMOVNT PARK
PHILADELPHIA

NVMBER 9
JANVARY, 1903

5 CENTS

Carl M. Muhly.

Entered, August 27, 1903, at Philadelphia, Pa., as second-class matter, under Act of Congress of July 16, 1894.

# FOLLOWING THE PRINCIPLES
# OF QUALITY AND INNOVATION

When Dalton Dorr died suddenly in February 1901, Barber was elected to succeed him as the Museum's curator. He continued to consult with Morris regarding most Museum matters, including the new Museum publication that Barber had proposed just weeks before Dorr's death: "I have made arrangements for devoting more time to collecting work and literary work, and it seems to me that there is need of a Museum publication, say a monthly paper, to be devoted to all subjects in which the Museum is interested. Such a publication ought to pay for itself, with possibly a little financial help at the outset, and would attract much attention to the Museum and give it standing among the great Museums of this country."[95] Accordingly, in January 1903 the Museum published its first number of the *Bulletin of the Pennsylvania Museum*, "for the purpose of bringing members of the corporation into closer touch with the work which is being done at the Museum,"[96] as well as to report on the institution's new acquisitions, installations, illustrated art handbooks in preparation, and Temple Fund purchases. The publication also included a plea for establishing similar purchase funds for "modern art glasswares" and other collections.[97] The *Bulletin* was published quarterly until 1919, then irregularly, sometimes more and sometimes less often, frequently serving as a collection handbook or an exhibition catalogue and typically as a vehicle for documenting new acquisitions (fig. 46). Philadelphia's was the first museum publication of its kind in the United States (followed shortly thereafter by the Museum of Fine Arts, Boston *Bulletin*), a fact of which Barber felt justly proud, reporting in 1911, "Other museums followed the example of the Pennsylvania Museum and at present there is scarcely an important public art museum in the United States which does not print its official organ."[98]

As curator, and later director, Barber was eager to professionalize the Museum, endeavoring to broaden its influence and build its collections. He first tackled housekeeping issues, from cleaning Memorial Hall to reclassifying, relabeling, and reinstalling the collections,[99] but he also set about building the size and importance of the Museum's collections by adding more specialized departments staffed with honorary curators. At Dorr's death in 1901 the Museum comprised five departments. Within a year Barber had added six more, including arms and armor; musical instruments; sculpture, marbles, and casts; furniture and woodwork; prints, manuscripts, book plates, and historic seals; and philately—with the hope that they would "prove an important feature in the educational work of the Museum."[100] Barber continued to take personal responsibility for the pottery and porcelain department, which he admittedly favored, years later explaining: "At the beginning of the present administration the Curator endeavored to find at least one department of art in which the Museum might hope to compete with or excel other Museums. The most promising field appeared to be ceramics and around the nucleus of the collection then in possession of the Museum, by filling in gap after gap, the present collection has been assembled, which is admitted to be, if not the largest, the most comprehensive and representative one in this country. . . . The collections include many wares which are not to be found in any other American or foreign museum."[101] The Museum's first "Art Handbook," written by Barber on *Tulip Ware of the Pennsylvania-German Potters*, was published in 1903 along with the first issue of the *Bulletin*.[102] Barber was also responsible for the establishment of a pottery department at the Museum school, writing Morris in late 1902: "I have been talking to Mr. Miller lately in regard to the advisability of establishing a Pottery School and I find that he is quite enthusiastic on the subject" (the department was established the following year).[103]

46. *Bulletin of the Pennsylvania Museum*, vol. 3, no. 9 (January 1, 1905)

Abetted and sometimes guided by Morris, Barber continued to acquire contemporary ceramics, telling Morris in 1902: "As I write, the Teco vase from Chicago has arrived and is the best piece of this ware which I have seen" (fig. 49).[104] Morris also continued to buy, offering many of his purchases to Barber for the Museum. "I had a wagon sent to your house," Barber wrote. "I am very much pleased with the contents. . . . There were in the boxes four pieces of Gustafsberg [sic] porcelain [fig. 48], two Rörstrand vases, and a Parian Group."[105] The Louisiana Purchase Exposition of 1904, better known as the Saint Louis World's Fair, provided Morris with ample opportunity for acquisition. Barber apparently was unable to attend and declined an invitation to accept an appointment as juror.[106] The museum committee, which had been chaired since 1897 by trustee John Story Jenks, voted Morris the use of the Temple and Museum Offertory funds for the purchase of art objects at the fair, with the hope, as Barber wrote, that he would "secure some fine things for us."[107] Morris outdid himself in Saint Louis, buying the latest and most advanced ceramics and glass from both the English and French exhibitions—works of James Powell and Sons and the Ruskin Pottery, and by the French artists Eugène Carrière, Auguste Delaherche, Taxile Doat, Émile Gallé, and André Fernand Thesmar. Sadly, only the masterwork by Gallé, a cased glass vase, cut, engraved, and decorated with an applied dragonfly (fig. 39), remains today in the Museum's collections, while a handsome example of Powell glass was added decades later. When the Gallé vase arrived in Philadelphia, Barber wrote Morris that he was "very much pleased with it. It is the best thing that has come from St. Louis, so far."[108]

Morris found an amiable and intelligent colleague in Jenks, who visited the Saint Louis fair and continued negotiations on behalf of the Museum after Morris had returned to Philadelphia. Descended from a colonial Quaker family and coproprietor of Randolph and Jenks, a leading cotton house in Philadelphia, Jenks was particularly interested in numismatics as well as Asian works of art. The previous

year, he and Morris had presented the Museum with "a series of antique wood carvings from dismantled palaces of Japan."[109] At the Saint Louis fair Jenks and Morris purchased seven examples, no longer in the Museum's collections, of contemporary Japanese metal. Jenks's letters to Morris from Saint Louis reveal a keen aesthetic sensibility. He describes a Japanese ivory figure of a woman sweeping and an "exquisite" lacquer panel with waves of platinum; the Gallé vase with a dragonfly, "a splendid specimen"; and "superb" enamel cups by Thesmar—"the red one is the finest," he noted. "I think that we had better secure it for the Museum."[110] Typical of Morris's appreciation for high-quality, innovative contemporary decorative arts was his interest in the simple, functional furniture designed for the Vereinigte Werkstätten für Kunst im Handwerk (United Workshops for Art in Craft), established in 1897 in Munich. "The German furniture exhibit is very beautiful," wrote Jenks to Morris from the fair, "Much obliged for calling my attention to it."[111] Although the Museum did not purchase any of the examples,[112] many years later it did acquire an important piece of furniture designed for the Vereinigte Werkstätten by Richard Riemerschmid (fig. 50) along with his stoneware jug and a colored woodcut by Peter Behrens (fig. 51).

During the first decade of the twentieth century, the "modern art glasswares" for which Barber sought special funding in the Museum's *Bulletin* were most consistently made by Tiffany. In the spring of 1905 the board approved the purchase of six pieces of Tiffany glass out of the Temple Fund (fig. 47); in 1908 a Tiffany cameo vase; and in 1912 eight pieces of Tiffany glass (fig. 55).[113] The negotiations over these and other purchases caused Morris and Barber to debate the Museum's collecting policies. In June 1904 W. H. Thomas, secretary and treasurer of Tiffany Furnaces, proposed sending Barber "fifty or sixty" pieces for review: "We regret that our exhibit was not in place at the time Mr. Morris was in Saint Louis, but the exhibit there is quite a small one and we doubt if it will answer the purpose of completing your collection, as well as one specially

47. Louis Comfort Tiffany : for Tiffany : Vase : c. 1905 : Favrile glass : H 13 1/8" : 1905-167 (cat. 192)

48. Gunnar Gunnarson Wennerburg : for Gustavsberg Porslinsfabrik : Vase : 1903 : enameled earthenware : H 5¹/₂" : 1903-1693 (cat. 211)

49. William J. Dodd : for Teco : Vase : c. 1902 : glazed earthenware : H 13³/₈" : 1902-922 (cat. 45)

selected."[114] On reading Thomas's letter, Morris wrote Barber that he liked the idea of buying "in wholesale quantities," although he thought it "pretty risky to have so many specimens sent over. They are delicate and liable to break." He suggested instead that Tiffany send "from time to time on approval specimens of their work as they make new attempts."[115] Barber then succinctly wrote Thomas that the Museum "would rather have *one* of your best productions than a *dozen* pieces of lesser merit."[116]

The principles of quality and innovation, both technical and aesthetic, were articulated by Morris in a letter to Barber the following year: "I think it would be the greatest mistake for us to decide without first visiting the [Tiffany] showroom or factory. . . . Do not let money enter into the question; what we want is the *very best first*; and then the *most distinctive*. Kindly, remember they are not going out of business and for that reason it will be better to buy from time to time their new productions rather than fill up our case at one time. I am so anxious to have a policy of making chronological collections. No one is doing it and some day I think our endeavor would be appreciated."[117] He subsequently emphasized, "I am . . . of the opinion that we should not purchase any article upon the sole opinion of the manufacturer."[118]

Barber did visit the Tiffany showroom in May 1905 and reported to Morris: "I went to New York last week to make the selection of Tiffany glass and was fortunate enough to meet Mr. Tiffany himself. I have selected some very beautiful and novel things. . . . Mr. Tiffany had a case of art pottery which he has been producing in a limited way, none of which has been put on the market and he did not wish to dispose of any of it. I induced him, however, to include two of the best pieces and if we want them, he will let us have them as a great favor."[119]

Meanwhile, Morris continued to buy Tiffany works both for himself and the Museum, including a piece of the new pottery of which Mr. Tiffany was so possessive. Morris sometimes reversed his opinion about a particular piece, as when he wrote Barber in 1908: "I have been thinking over the small Tiffany vase. Before it is too late to come to a decision regarding it, place it alongside the other specimens and I am inclined to think you will agree with me that it is not interesting enough for us and will rather detract from the collection."[120]

62

Opposite : **50. Richard Riemerschmid** : for Vereinigte Werkstätten für Kunst im Handwerk : Chair : 1907 : oak, leather : H 30⅝" : 1991-17-1 (cat. 159)    Above : **51. Peter Behrens** : *The Kiss* : 1899 : color woodcut : H (image) 10¾" : 1976–78–1 (cat. 16)

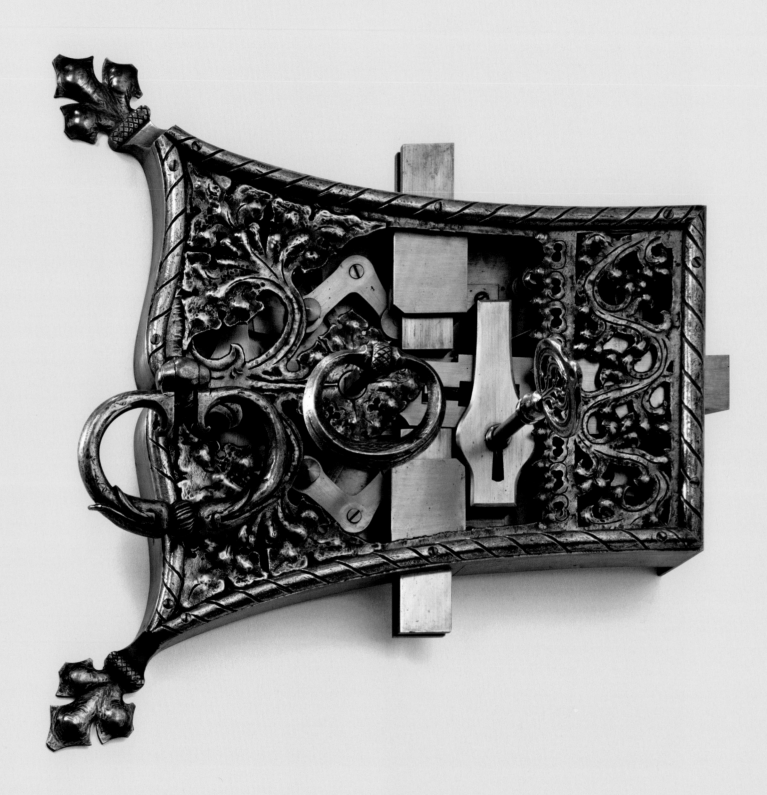

100. *Annual Report, Pennsylvania Museum and School of Industrial Art* [year ending December 31, 1902] (Philadelphia, 1902), p. 19.

101. Barber, "Decennial Report," p. 2.

102. Barber made a special plea for a publication fund in that year's annual report: "Of even greater importance than the acquisition of new material, after a museum has grown to the proportions of this, is the publication of original works which shall be accepted as authoritative contributions to the literature of art. A moderate fund would enable the Curator to carry on this important work without embarrassment." *Annual Report, Pennsylvania Museum and School of Industrial Art* [year ending December 31, 1903] (Philadelphia, 1903), p. 19.

103. Barber to Morris, December 29, 1902, Barber Records, Correspondence with Morris et al.

104. Barber to Morris, November 25, 1902, Barber Records, Correspondence with Morris et al.

105. Barber to Morris, December 1, 1903, Barber Records, Correspondence with Morris et al.

106. Barber to Morris, September 19, 1904, Barber Records, Correspondence with Morris et al.

107. Barber to Morris, June 7, 1904, Barber Records, Correspondence with Morris et al.

108. Barber to Morris, January 28, 1905, Barber Records, Correspondence with Morris et al.

109. *Annual Report*, [1903], p. 13.

110. John Story Jenks to Morris, September 15, 1904, Accession Files, Registrar.

111. Ibid.

112. John Wanamaker, however, acquired twenty-one German interiors for display in his Philadelphia store.

113. Board of Trustees Records, Minutes, May 11, 1905; June 8, 1905; January 9, 1908; January, 11, 1912; and October 10, 1912.

114. W. H. Thomas to Barber, June 27, 1904, Barber Records, Correspondence.

115. Morris to Barber, July 1, 1904, Barber Records, Correspondence with Morris et al.

116. Barber to Thomas, July 1, 1904, Barber Records, Correspondence; emphases in the original.

117. Morris to Barber, April 1, 1905, Barber Records, Correspondence with Morris et al; emphases in the original.

118. Morris to Barber, April 20, 1905, Barber Records, Correspondence with Morris et al.

119. Barber to Morris, May 4, 1905, Barber Records, Correspondence with Morris et al.

120. Morris to Barber, January 7, 1908, Barber Records, Correspondence with Morris et al.

121. Morris to Barber, December 2, 1910, Barber Records, Correspondence with Morris et al.

122. Barber to Morris, December 3, 1910, Barber Records, Correspondence with Morris et al.

123. Barber to Morris, May 4, 1911, Barber Records, Correspondence with Morris et al. Morris responded: "I particularly liked *one* piece of new Japan which could be worth having in a *new* collection. I should love to have it in my private little collection but I propose to resist temptation." Morris to Barber, May 5, 1911, Barber Records, Correspondence with Morris et al.; emphases in the original.

124. Barber to Morris, February 27, 1911, Barber Records, Correspondence with Morris et al.

125. Board of Trustees Records, Museum Committee, Minutes, March 8, 1911; and *Bulletin of the Pennsylvania Museum*, vol. 11, no. 42 (April 1913): p. 35.

126. The *Christian Science Monitor* described the collection as "one of the finest of its kind in America"; "Philadelphia Art," *Christian Science Monitor*, May 5, 1916, p. 8.

127. Contrary to published accounts, John McIlhenny, father of John D. McIlhenny, did not invent the gas meter but rather patented in 1895 a gas valve that helped make his company successful, providing the basis upon which the family's fortune was built.

128. [Edwin Atlee Barber], "On the Cooperation of Public Museums," *Bulletin of the Pennsylvania Museum*, vol. 3, no. 10 (April 1905): p. 38.

129. Edwin Atlee Barber to Herman C. Bumpus, May 14, 1906, Barber Records, Correspondence.

130. "If any arrangement is made to send Dr. Barber to Europe this summer, I will be glad to subscribe $100 toward the expenses"; Morris to Jenks, January 4, 1910, Barber Records, Correspondence. The board authorized Barber's trip at its meeting on May 12, 1910, along with the use of "the available fund of the Temple Trust . . . for the purchase of objects for the Museum, should desirable examples be found"; Board of Trustees Records, Minutes, May 12, 1910.

131. Morris to Barber, May 18, 1910, Barber Records, Correspondence with Morris et al.

132. Barber to Morris, April 27, 1910, Barber Records, Correspondence with Morris et al.

133. Edwin Atlee Barber, "Report of the Director of the Museum to the Board of Trustees of the Pennsylvania Museum and School of Industrial Art on the Museums Visited by Him during His Recent European Trip," November 1, 1910, annotated typescript, Edwin Atlee Barber Papers.

134. Justus Brinckmann, *Führer durch das Hamburgische Museum für Kunst und Gewerbe.Zugleich ein Handbuch der Geschichte des Kunstgewerbes* (Hamburg: Verlag des Museums für Kunst und Gewerbe, 1894), pp. v, vii; my translation.

135. Barber to Morris, August 11, 1910, Barber Records, Correspondence with Morris et al.

136. Barber to Morris, August 16, 1910, Barber Records, Correspondence with Morris et al.

137. Barber to Morris, October 26, 1910, Barber Records, Correspondence with Morris et al.

138. Morris to Barber, July 28, 1911, Barber Records, Correspondence with Morris et al.; emphases in the original.

139. Barber to Morris, July 29, 1911, Barber Records, Correspondence with Morris et al.

140. Morris to Barber, October 13, 1911; emphases in the original.

141. Morris to Barber, July 24, 1912, Barber Records, Correspondence with Morris et al.

142. Morris to Barber, March 18, 1914, Barber Records, Correspondence with Morris et al.

143. Morris to Barber, July 16, 1915, Barber Records, Correspondence with Morris et al.; emphases in the original.

144. Barber to Morris, July 17, 1915, Barber Records, Correspondence with Morris et al.

145. Board of Trustees Records, Museum Committee, Minutes, November 1, 1915.

146. *Bulletin of the Pennsylvania Museum*, vol. 13, no. 52 (October 1915): p. 62.

147. Board of Trustees Records, Museum Committee, Minutes, January 2, 1917.

148. "In Memoriam," *Bulletin of the Pennsylvania Museum*, vol. 15, no. 57 (January 1917): p. 1.

# 1916-
# 1964

assistant curator;[40] Downs was then working at the Museum of Fine Arts, Boston and additionally employed in the design departments of "leading furniture manufacturers" in New York.[41] During Woodhouse's two-year tenure, the Museum acquired a contemporary tapestry designed by Gustave Jaulmes for the Gobelins manufactory, representing American army units passing Independence Hall in Philadelphia, on their way to France, a gift from the republic of France to the city of Philadelphia. The Museum's new Print Room[42] hosted a sale exhibition, *Etchings and Engravings by Contemporary Artists of Holland*, which brought the Museum publicity and about $1,000 in revenue.[43]

Meanwhile, from the spring of 1924 to June 1925, McIlhenny sought a Museum director, courting Fiske Kimball (fig. 64), a Harvard-trained architect and architectural historian (B.A. and M.Arch., with a Ph.D. from the University of Michigan) who in 1923 had left the University of Virginia, where he headed the department of art and architecture, to create a graduate program at New York University's Institute of Fine Arts. As Kimball remembered a decade later, his first reaction on seeing the Museum in Philadelphia and its collections in 1924 was mixed:

> The Pennsylvania Museum . . . had occupied since 1876 the art building of the Centennial Exposition, Memorial Hall. . . . Few other American public buildings of that date held their own so well. In the public mind, however, it passed as a stuffy relic of an unfashionable era. . . .
>
> The Museum had stressed the industrial aspect, both in the reading of its title and in its collections. Indeed, naturally enough—as there were then no museums of industry in the United States—industrial products had been admitted which had little to do with industrial art in any aesthetic sense. . . . Much had been done to reform the Museum, although as a whole it still presented a forlorn and unpromising aspect.[44]

Kimball refused McIlhenny's initial offer, as he had only recently arrived at his position in New York: "It is indeed with great regret that I have to inform you that it seems best that I remain here. My associates and superiors seem to feel it would be disloyal for me to desert the ship after such a brief time at the helm."[45] When asked again a year later, however, Kimball accepted the post of director in Philadelphia, subsequently recalling: "This time the New York authorities gave me their blessing. . . . The new Museum building had meanwhile advanced notably [figs. 63, 65]. . . . [McIlhenny] had made it a condition that I should go abroad, where I had not been for a dozen years, before taking up my duties in September."[46]

Like Edwin Atlee Barber's visit before him, Kimball's trip to Europe impressed the new director with the "antique architectural features" installed at German museums, which "added greatly to the effect and gave an idea of the ensemble in their periods."[47] Completing the new Museum building and fitting it with period architecture and objects in chronological and geographic sequence would be Kimball's life work as director over a thirty-year period. In addition, he became deeply involved with the restoration and furnishing of the eighteenth- and nineteenth-century houses in Fairmount Park that were under the custodianship of the Museum. Kimball regarded the park houses as Philadelphia's unique artistic resource, illustrating the

Opposite : **63.** The Museum under construction : July 11, 1926    Above : **64.** Fiske Kimball : Museum director, 1925–55

development of American architecture and decoration alongside the Museum's own collections. As a specialist in eighteenth-century American architecture, Kimball held the park houses, as well as the Museum's American period rooms, particularly dear to his heart. He also announced soon after his arrival that it was the Museum's "local duty . . . to buy fine examples of Philadelphia craftsmanship as they become available."[48]

John D. McIlhenny did not live to see the opening of the Museum's new building in 1928 (fig. 71), and died shortly after Kimball's return to Philadelphia from Europe in November 1925.[49] In McIlhenny's place, Eli Kirk Price became Museum president and John Story Jenks chair of the museum committee.

What Kimball must have seen in Europe, although curiously he made no mention of it, was the great International Exposition of Decorative and Industrial Arts, which also featured modern architecture, then being held in Paris. Woodhouse, however, had already written McIlhenny in March 1925 that "good old Mrs. Blankenburg broke into the Museum's proceedings to announce the many attractions of [the exposition] and that you were going to finance one professor going abroad, that Mrs. McFadden Brinton has financed another, that the Women's Committee were going to finance a third and that they greatly wished to send a fourth."[50] As had been the case for the late nineteenth-century international exhibitions, the board seemed to feel it most necessary to send abroad staff from the school, rather than from the Museum, to see contemporary international decorative arts. Moreover, the

Above and opposite, left to right : **65. Attributed to Julian Abele** : Perspective of the Museum's Stair Hall : c. 1927 : crayon on tracing paper : H 16" : PDP-1085 (cat. 000)    66. Catalogue for the American exhibition featuring selections from the Paris Exposition of 1925 (Washington, D.C.: American Association of Museums, 1925)    67. **Edgar Brandt** : Forged iron console table, mirror, and standing lamps, with bronze statuette by Max Blondat : from the Paris Exposition of 1925 : on view at the Museum in 1926

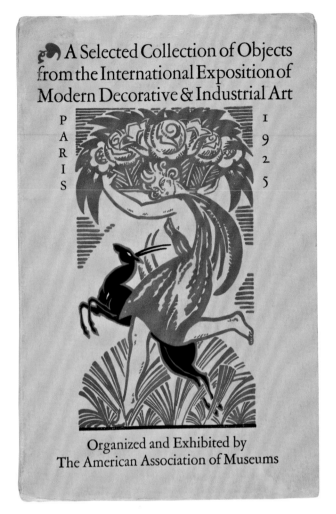

Museum acquired no objects from the exhibition for its collections, either by gift or by purchase, as it certainly would have if John T. Morris had still been alive. Board members and others might be forgiven, however, since the United States had officially declined to participate in the exhibition, a government commission determining that American manufacturers and craftsmen had "almost nothing to exhibit in the modern spirit."[51] Still, architect George Howe was among the Philadelphians who did visit the exposition, returning deeply impressed by Le Corbusier's Pavilion de l'Esprit Nouveau—a radical experiment in mass-production building and furnishing.

Although the curatorial staff of the Museum seems largely to have ignored the exhibition in Paris, a selection of its objects traveled to Philadelphia the following year (figs.

66, 67) and, as Kimball noted in his second annual report, "attracted much serious attention from students and designers."[52] The objects in the exhibition had been selected from those at the 1925 Paris venue by Charles Richards, former director of the Cooper Union in New York and at the time director of the American Association of Museums, which circulated the show to nine American cities. The show provided many Philadelphians with their first exposure to the new, international French Art Deco style as well as the opportunity to acquire examples of it, but apparently none did. However, Joseph Downs, who had taken up the position of assistant curator for decorative arts around the time that Kimball became director, wrote an article about the contemporary decorative arts exhibition in the November 1926 issue of the Museum's *Bulletin*, in which he argued: "It is perhaps to the designer and manufacturer that this exhibition will make the widest appeal, since a solution of the problems of industrial arts is presented in terms of modern life. In America, where architecture has advanced by leaps and bounds to meet logically the demands of the present day, little or no effort has been made to develop the decorative arts in a similar manner. Into diminutive apartments and office buildings . . . have gone the copies of the past."[53]

But three years later, in early 1929, Downs could boast of the Museum's first American acquisition "in the contemporary style," a buffet by the New York designer Eugene Schoen (fig. 68) that had been given that year by the Modern Club of Philadelphia, a women's service organization. Downs wrote that the buffet represented "the first link toward a collection of modern decorative arts and is particularly welcome owing to the lack of any example of this period in the Museum's collection."[54] The previous fall, the Museum had hosted the AFA's *International Exhibition of Ceramic Art* (funded by the General Education Board, a Rockefeller philanthropy), which comprised some four hundred pieces and was, Downs indicated, "the first of many [exhibitions] which the Museum plans in its programme of coordinating the problems of art with industry in Philadelphia."[55] Once again, no acquisitions for the Museum resulted from the exhibition, although Kimball observed that "public interest has been very considerable, as evidenced by attendance, by sale of catalogues and of objects."[56]

These exhibitions of contemporary decorative arts were only footnotes in the history of the Museum during the later 1920s, as the board and Kimball were galvanized in their efforts to complete and open the new city building— which was known at least from the winter of 1924–25 as the Philadelphia Museum of Art.[57] Despite reductions in state appropriations to the Museum, its president Eli Kirk Price proved himself a mighty fund-raiser. There were increases in revenue, gifts to the endowment, and special contributions encouraged by Kimball for the purchase of

objects for the collections. An organized effort to raise approximately two million dollars was concluded in 1928 and covered "the cost of obtaining and erecting in the Museum an adequate number of original interiors of rooms, in which to display paintings, sculptures, furniture, curtains, china, silver and glass of the same period and country, and to create the nucleus of an endowment fund for the future operation of the Museum on the greatly extended scale required by the new building."[58] Price believed that an endowment of $15 million was vitally necessary to pay for installation of the architectural elements and objects Kimball was acquiring, as well as to complete construction of the Museum's still unfinished interior for study collections and administrative offices. However, it was only five decades later, in 1978, that the Museum's total endowment would reach Price's goal.[59]

The rate at which Kimball acquired period architecture during the later 1920s was nothing short of astonishing; in 1926 alone he obtained a room from the Powel House in Philadelphia, as well as architectural elements from the Derby House in Salem, Massachusetts; from the town of Millbach in Lebanon County, Pennsylvania; and from Treaty House (now known as "New Place") in Upminster, England. Two years later Kimball purchased thirteen major architectural elements, including a medieval stone portal from the abbey church of Saint-Laurent, in central France; a cloister from the abbey church of Saint-Génis-des Fontaines; a seventeenth-century Dutch interior; two eighteenth-century French rooms; four eighteenth-century English rooms; and a ceremonial teahouse of about 1917 from Tokyo. His plan for the new Museum building was revealed in the October 1927 issue of the *Bulletin* as

a series of galleries ranged in historic order, a selection of masterpieces in painting and sculpture along with the furniture and other objects of their own time. By following only this "main street" of the Museum, the visitor will retrace the great historic pageant of the evolution of art. . . . The new building provides such

68. Eugene Schoen : for Schmieg, Hungate & Kotzian : Buffet : 1927 : Macassar ebony, rosewood, walnut, oak, and cherry woods and veneers, brass : W 6' : 1929-45-1a,b (cat. 174)

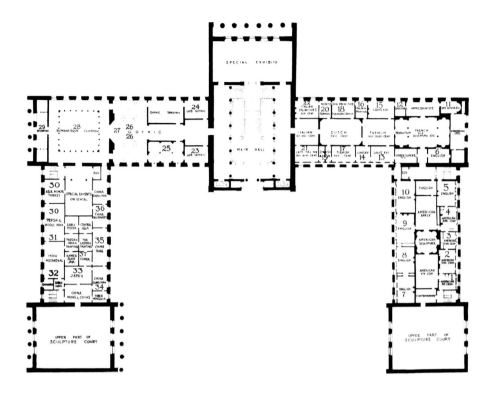

advantages of space, design and flexibility as hitherto have not been available, at one time, in an American museum. It will allow the devotion of the entire main floor to the masterpieces and period rooms which are of greatest popular interest, and of another floor to the multitude of objects constituting the study collections, which are of primary interest to the student, the manufacturer and the collector.[60]

These specialized study exhibits were to be arranged according to material and technique, as they had been in Memorial Hall under Barber's directorship. Kimball's proposed floor plan of the new building illustrated his historical chain of galleries and period rooms on the second floor (fig. 69).[61] Room 11, labeled Art Nouveau, was intended for French nineteenth-century objects, "style of Bing, glass of Lalique and Gallé, ceramics of Delaherche, etc."[62] The display of modern if not contemporary French decorative arts, along with Impressionist and Expressionist paintings and French nineteenth-century sculpture, thus concluded a suite of historic French rooms and galleries. Kimball's plan also indicated that the English and American exhibition

galleries and period rooms would similarly culminate in a "contemporary" gallery, adjacent to nineteenth-century American woodwork and works of art. It is clear that Kimball intended this art historical sequence in the Museum to finish in the present, and he provided, even if not liberally, space to house contemporary works. In this spirit the Museum years later acquired by gift a twentieth-century American period room—a library (as well as a music room) from the home of Curtis and Nellie Lee Bok in Gulph Mills, Pennsylvania, with woodwork and furniture by Philadelphia artist-craftsman Wharton H. Esherick (fig. 70). Kimball had noted in 1926 that "compared to Museums in many smaller cities our income for purchases from Museum funds is still relatively small,"[63] and in the following year that "any active purchasing of portable objects has been suspended in favor of the acquisition of these major decorative and structural elements—carved doorways, ceilings and whole interiors."[64] He nevertheless successfully exploited the economic boom of the 1920s in Philadelphia and the nation, acquiring within five years all of the American, European, and Asian architectural elements, woodwork, and interiors necessary to realize his great historical plan for the second-floor galleries.

Above : 69. Fiske Kimball's floor plan for the new Museum building on Fairmount : c. 1927   Opposite : 70. Wharton H. Esherick : Fireplace and Doorway from the Library of the Curtis and Nellie Lee Bok House (Gulph Mills, Pennsylvania) : 1936 : oak, stone, copper : L 16' : 1989-1,2 (cat. 58)

# A MOVE TO
# FAIRMOUNT

The new Museum opened to the public on March 26, 1928, with ten eighteenth-century American and English period rooms on view in the northeast wing. For his "indefatigable and excellent work in connection with the installation of the collections at Fairmount," Joseph Downs was promoted to curator of decorative arts.[65] The building was described by Richard Bach of the Metropolitan Museum of Art as "a Philadelphian Acropolis" that required "a goodly assortment of superlatives," and as "a model of Greek Ionic architecture" that "should please any classicist."[66] A temple to the arts, Philadelphia's new museum, if not modern in style, was a grand summation of nineteenth-century nationalistic ideas and historicizing forms, consistently and broadly applied (fig. 71).

The taste for modernism in general was nonetheless advancing in Philadelphia and elsewhere during the 1920s, despite opposition by the Philadelphia Art Teachers Association and other reactionary groups.[67] Earl Horter was one of a group of avant-garde artists and collectors in Philadelphia, along with painters Arthur B. Carles, Henry McCarter, and Franklin Watkins, who promoted modern art to collectors—including Carroll S. Tyson, Jr., and Anna Warren Ingersoll (both of whom were also artists); R. Sturgis Ingersoll; Vera White (also an artist) and her husband, Samuel S. White III; Alexander Lieberman; and George Howe.[68] The inaugural exhibition at the new building on Fairmount included contemporary paintings by Georges Braque, Henri Matisse, Pablo Picasso, and others lent by Horter, Sturgis Ingersoll, Lieberman, Tyson, and the Whites (who later became trustees of the Museum).[69] Sturgis Ingersoll joined the museum committee in 1932 and Carroll Tyson the following year; Ingersoll was elected to the Museum's board in 1938. Descended from a distinguished family of well-born and well-educated Philadelphia lawyers, including Jared Ingersoll, a signer of the Constitution, Sturgis and his sister Anna were among the Museum's most important advocates for acquisitions of modern painting and sculpture (see fig. 73).

Fiske Kimball was certainly aware of developments in modern art beyond Philadelphia. His papers preserved at the Museum include the second annual report for the Harvard Society for Contemporary Art,[70] which had been formed at Harvard College in the winter of 1928–29 by three students—Lincoln Kirstein, John Walker, and Edward Warburg—to exhibit and sell contemporary works, a project that continued until 1934. The society's first exhibition, in February 1929, featured American paintings, sculptures, and works on paper, along with objects by American designer Donald Deskey and others;[71] the second exhibition, *The School of Paris*, also

Above : **71.** The Museum with unfinished courtyard and ramping walkways : c. 1928   Opposite : **72. Alphonse Mucha** : Boutique Fouquet : 1901 : Musée Carnavalet : Paris

held that year, included lacquers by Jean Dunand and glass by René Lalique and Maurice Marinot.[72] Nine months later, the Museum of Modern Art was founded in New York—modeled on the Harvard Society for Contemporary Art—by collectors Lillie P. Bliss and Abby Aldrich Rockefeller (both sustaining members of the society) and Mary Quinn Sullivan, with the cooperation of patrons, collectors, and dealers who had been enlisted in the Harvard experiment. The Modern's first director, Alfred H. Barr, Jr., was a former graduate student at Harvard University and member of and unofficial advisor to the Harvard Society for Contemporary Art. Linking the modernists of Cambridge, New York, and Philadelphia was Paul J. Sachs, member of the great New York banking family, professor of fine arts and assistant director of the Fogg Art Museum at Harvard, trustee of the Harvard Society, and founding trustee of the Museum of Modern Art. Sachs regularly brought his students to Philadelphia as part of his legendary course on museum methods, including a visit in 1930 after Kimball had advised him about "newer" collections of modern art, such as those of Sturgis Ingersoll, Carroll Tyson, and S. S. White.[73] Several of Sachs's students eventually joined the Museum staff, among them, Henry P. McIlhenny, only surviving son of the Museum's former president John D. McIlhenny. A student of fine arts at Harvard from 1929 to 1933, as well as an advisee of Sachs, Henry would become the curator of decorative arts at the Philadelphia Museum of Art, but he must have observed the Harvard Society for Contemporary Art from a distance, as he was more comfortable with the acceptably modern than the avant-garde or controversial. In 1934 Kimball reported that "John D. McIlhenny, in his day, bought old pictures, but his son Henry now buys nothing but moderns, and the same is true of everybody else."[74]

In March 1929 Kimball traveled to Europe to continue his search for period rooms and related elements, as the institution had received large specific subscriptions for three items: a French Gothic chapel, a Directoire or Adam interior, and a "modern French room."[75] After Kimball's departure, acting director Horace Jayne reported more precisely that Kimball would be taking steps "toward securing designs by one of the leading French decorative designers, for the room subscribed for by Mr. Louis Page, to be conceived as something similar to a shop interior, of refinement and dignity, so as to permit the display not only of furniture and painting, but in vitrines, of objects of minor art."[76] However, when Kimball revealed in September 1929 that he had been negotiating "the purchase of materials of a shop in the rue Royale, Paris, designed by Alphonse Mucha, 1900,"[77] he already knew that the museum committee would not readily approve the purchase, as he had earlier written the vendor:

Since leaving Paris and arriving here I have had your shop very constantly in mind, and have worked more than you may imagine toward its acquisition by the Museum. Our friend [Charles] Richards, I am glad to say, joined with me in urging its importance and its desirability for us. It will scarcely surprise you however, to learn that he and I, in our enthusiasm for it, are more than a little in advance of the conservatism of a number of our Museum Trustees, and that it has not been easy to persuade them to favor it. The purchase would be one of those courageous, prophetic actions which are so difficult to take when a number of persons are concerned.[78]

GALLERY OF MODERN ART

**PENNSYLVANIA MUSEUM OF ART**

LOAN EXHIBITION OF

CONTEMPORARY PAINTING

AND SCULPTURE

FROM THE COLLECTIONS OF

MISS ANNA WARREN INGERSOLL

AND

MR. & MRS. R. STURGIS INGERSOLL

PHILADELPHIA

NOVEMBER 4—DECEMBER 6, 1933

THE MUSEUM AT FAIRMOUNT IS OPEN ON MONDAY, WEDNESDAY AND SATURDAY FROM 10 TO 5; ON SUNDAY FROM 1 TO 5

As Kimball had feared, the matter was tabled by the committee, to be brought up later by the director at his discretion, and sadly disappeared thereafter from the records of the Museum. The shop in question had been designed by the Czech artist Alphonse Mucha for the Parisian jeweler Georges Fouquet, a unique commission of extravagantly rich carving, stained glass, mosaics, and bronze fittings that would have given the Museum the most important French Art Nouveau interior outside France. Instead, in 1941 the interior was acquired by the Musée Carnavalet in Paris, where it can be seen today (fig. 72).

Despite the conservatism of the museum committee, in November 1929 its chair, John Story Jenks, "presented certain considerations regarding the situation of the Museum in respect to works of modern art," and the committee "resolved to recommend to the Trustees the creation of a Committee on Modern Art to assist in securing for the Museum representative works."[79] The new committee included Jenks himself and Kimball, along with artists Adolphe Borie and Carroll Tyson, architect George Howe, Sturgis Ingersoll, and Charles Richards (recently appointed executive secretary of the New York Museum of Science and Industry and Kimball's supporter regarding the Mucha/Fouquet shop). Although the modern art committee had been established, according to Kimball, for the purpose of devoting "adequate space . . . to the work of contemporary artists"[80]—defined largely as painting and sculpture—Jenks, Howe, and Richards brought their own ideas about modern art and design into the mix. While studying art in Paris in the spring of 1928, Jenks's daughter, Ann, had met Alexey Brodovitch, the Russian-born art director of the Maison Blanche department store.[81] Convinced of Brodovitch's talent, Jenks persuaded the designer to give notice at Maison Blanche, uproot his family, and come to America to accept a teaching post in advertising design at the Pennsylvania Museum school. Brodovitch assumed the position in the fall of 1930,[82] bringing advanced European graphic approaches to the school and subsequently to *Harper's Bazaar* magazine,

73. Catalogue for an exhibition from the collections of Anna Ingersoll and Marion and Sturgis Ingersoll : November 4–December 6, 1933

where his use of new typefaces, photography, subtle color combinations, and clear, open spaces revolutionized American advertising and editorial design. He was recognized as a gifted and generous teacher, assisting photographers Irving Penn and Ben Rose, among others.

As modernism began to gain a foothold at the Museum and school, Kimball struggled to complete the medieval section of the building, adding curatorial staff to help him develop and install collections there (fig. 74). New staff members included medievalist Francis Henry Taylor and Henri Marceau, who was named curator of fine arts in 1929, the same year he also succeeded Hamilton Bell as curator of the John G. Johnson Collection.[83] Affluent, Oxford-educated, and well-traveled, Henry Clifford arrived at the Museum in 1930 to become Marceau's assistant. Joseph Downs, meanwhile, heroically and intelligently carried on as curator of decorative arts, a position vital to Kimball's program of installing period architecture and interiors on Fairmount.

74. Senior staff at the Museum's East Entrance : June 4, 1929 : left to right : Horace H. F. Jayne, Francis Henry Taylor, Joseph Downs, J. Stogdell Stokes, Fiske Kimball, Paul H. Rea, and Erling Pedersen

# AN ECONOMIC CRISIS

The effects of the stock market crash in October 1929 and the ensuing Great Depression were not felt immediately at the Museum. In May 1930 the annual report provided an optimistic account of the most expensive acquisition in the institution's history: "During the year an opportunity occurred of securing the well-known Foulc Collection of late Gothic and early Renaissance objects of French and Italian art and the obtaining of the funds requisite to complete its purchase is going forward satisfactorily with every prospect of success."[84] It would take some twenty-two years to repay the several bank loans as well as a group of benefactors who had advanced the down payment on the purchase price of $1,100,000;[85] but by the close of the 1930 fiscal year, $654,412 had been subscribed by 353 donors toward the collection's purchase.[86] Individuals who wanted to make an impressive gift to the Museum could "buy" objects from the Foulc Collection, ranging from a seventeenth-century set of wrought-iron fireplace tools ($50) to a complete stone choir screen ($150,000; fig. 75), with each gift then transferred from storage to the exhibition galleries, where it was appropriately credited to the donor.[87] A number of objects from the collection were installed in the Museum's medieval section when it opened to the public less than a year later, in March 1931, Price proudly reporting that "this important period in the history of art has been so successfully done, that visitors to the Museum are unanimous in stating that a real atmosphere of the Middle Ages seems to have been created, which is far beyond anything hitherto achieved in other museums."[88] Preceding the Metropolitan Museum of Art's Cloisters building by seven years, Philadelphia's exhibition of Romanesque and Gothic architecture, interiors, and objects was then unmatched in the United States, reflecting "great credit" on the curator,

Francis Henry Taylor, according to Kimball.[89] Consequently, it came as no surprise when two months after the opening of the medieval section, Taylor resigned to assume the directorship of the Worcester Art Museum, in Massachusetts, later becoming director of the Metropolitan. That spring Kimball hired two young protégés of Paul Sachs, A.M. students at Harvard, to take on some of Taylor's responsibilities, including Calvin S. Hathaway, who became secretary to the director and editor of the *Bulletin*, and Beaumont Newhall, lecturer in education.

By early 1931 the museum committee was forced to acknowledge the severe economic downturn, although the momentum for modernism in general proceeded. Kimball described the acquisition of two paintings, Pierre-Auguste Renoir's portrait of Mme Renoir (1885; purchased with Elkins Fund income[90]) and the Museum's first Picasso, *Woman with Loaves* (1906; given by Charles E. Ingersoll at the behest of his son, Sturgis) as proof that the Museum was "alive to modern movements" (fig. 76).[91] In addition, Kimball applied to and received funding from the Carnegie Corporation of New York for an experimental branch museum to be located

Opposite : **75. Artist/maker unknown** (France) : Choir Screen from the Chapel of the Château of Pagny (detail) : 1536–38 : marble, alabaster : H 18' 9" : 1930-1-84a–d (cat. 10)    Above : **76. Pablo Ruiz y Picasso** : *Woman with Loaves* : 1906 : oil on canvas : H 39 3/16" : 1931-7-1 (cat. 150)

93

at the Sixty-ninth Street Arts and Crafts Community Center in Upper Darby, just west of Philadelphia, a site that would help to assess the value of branch museums, to be organized in a way similar to the existing system of branch libraries. In their letter to the corporation, Price and Kimball noted that the branch museum also should promote "the art interest of the local community" through exhibitions "specially adapted to the needs of the community" and visits by "outside personalities of a stimulating character."[92] Upon the recommendation of Frederick P. Keppel, president of the Carnegie Corporation, Kimball hired architect and educator Philip N. Youtz to run the suburban Sixty-ninth Street site as its curator (fig. 77). Among the exhibitions on view at the branch museum during its first year was a show on American industrial art, circulated by the AFA (see page 99).

Keppel and Carnegie were interested in industrial art, Keppel sharing with Kimball his outline for a report titled "The Arts and Recent Social Changes," in which he argued that "the substitution of the craftsman by the machine need not result, and as a matter of fact has not resulted, in lower standards of beauty in manufactured articles, but has undoubtedly changed the character of these standards."[93] In early 1931 Kimball too was thinking about contemporary industrial design, writing to the AFA that the Museum had been considering "an American manufacturer's exhibition, stressing Philadelphia products, not unlike the Manufacturers' show held annually at the Metropolitan Museum."[94] In fact, exhibitions held in the winter and spring of 1931–32 marked the Museum's greatest commitment to contemporary art and design during Kimball's long tenure as director, and members of the Museum's modern art committee assisted in all of them. The first exhibition, *Living Artists*,[95] opened in November 1931 and consisted of paintings and sculptures selected and installed by committee members Adolphe Borie, Sturgis Ingersoll, and Carroll Tyson, with

Ingersoll lending paintings by Marc Chagall and Henri Matisse as well as a Matisse sculpture.

In February 1932 curator Joseph Downs opened his monumental exhibition of industrial design, *Design for the Machine: Contemporary Industrial Art*,[96] again with the help of modern art committee members, in this case Charles Richards and George Howe (who with his partner, William E. Lescaze, was also an exhibitor). Richards outlined

the exhibition program in a catalogue that had been designed by the Museum school's Alexey Brodovitch (fig. 78): "The special qualities of the machine as a tool are speed, accuracy and strength. . . . In consequence, the aesthetic problem facing the designer for the machine is twofold: first, to determine the limits beyond which the machine or process should not be required to function; second, to determine the artistic principles that should govern the design of repetitive production. Both of these considerations make for simplicity of form and the elimination of all but extremely reserved functional ornament."[97] To plan the exhibition Downs collaborated with the American Union of Decorative Artists and Craftsmen, established in 1928; Brodovitch and Howe were members of the group, as

Above and opposite, left to right : 77. The Museum's Sixty-ninth Street branch : Upper Darby, Pennsylvania : 1931    78. *Design for the Machine* (Philadelphia: Philadelphia Museum of Art, 1932) : cover illustration by Alexey Brodovitch    79. *Modern Architecture: International Exhibition* (New York: Museum of Modern Art, 1932)

were the well-known industrial designers Donald Deskey, Gilbert Rohde, Walter Dorwin Teague, Kem Weber, and Russel Wright. Rohde designed a man's study to display at the Museum and equipped it with a contemporary furniture line he had created for Heywood-Wakefield, the first modern furniture produced by the firm (fig. 82).[98] Downs counted 225 designers, manufacturers, and distributors represented in the Philadelphia exhibition, and declared: "Whether it be the shop front designed by Walter

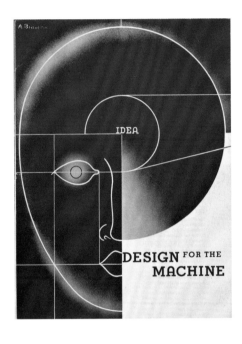 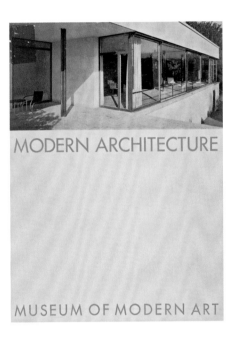

Dorwin Teague, at the beginning of the exhibition [fig. 80], the drawing room by Howe and Lescaze just beyond [fig. 81], or the eight rooms of a complete house devised by as many artists which follow, even the person who can see little of value in mass production should find much here to admire and remember."[99] And so the public and press did, Kimball noting that the exhibition had attracted "a very large attendance and wide favorable comment."[100] Reviews of the exhibition were carried in the local and national press, including the *San Francisco Chronicle,* the *Chicago Post,* and the *New York Times.* A large illustrated spread appeared in the *New York Times Magazine,* where the "comprehensive" exhibition was described as "graphically" demonstrating the aesthetic advances of contemporary

design, and lauded for the inclusion of models of large-scale machines, including an ocean liner, an automobile, a locomotive, and two airplanes.[101] Another publication pointed out the advantages of displaying contemporary design in room settings, next to ensembles from earlier eras: "Immediately adjoining the galleries where this exhibition is held are the museum's historic period rooms where the visitor may observe and appreciate by contrast, the deathless elements of handcraftsmen of the past—their period furniture, ceramics, paintings, sculptures and metal-work."[102]

Ten days after the close of *Design for the Machine,* in March 1932 *Modern Architecture: International Exhibition* arrived at the Philadelphia Museum of Art directly from the newly founded department of architecture at the Museum of Modern Art in New York, where the show had introduced Americans to the radical European buildings of Le Corbusier, Walter Gropius, Ludwig Mies van der Rohe, and J. J. P. Oud that are now landmarks of twentieth-century modernism (fig. 79).[103] Furniture and objects by these architects, among them Mies's tubular steel and cane chair (fig. 85) and works by Bauhaus designer Wilhelm Wagenfeld, would later enter the collection. Among the few Americans included in the exhibition were Howe and Lescaze, represented by their nearly completed Philadelphia Saving Fund Society Building—the first modern International Style skyscraper to be built in the United States, with its strip windows, thin curtain walls, and dependence on modern materials (fig. 83). Beyond this progressive architectural vocabulary, the tower was heralded for its pioneering mechanical and circulation systems, including escalators, high-rise elevators, and thermostatically controlled heat and air-conditioning. Howe and Lescaze designed every aspect of the building,

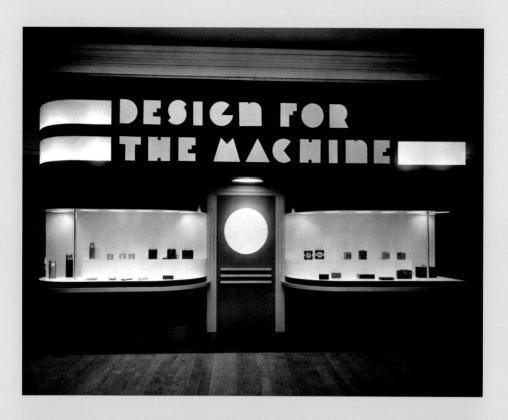

**Design for the Machine : 1932**

Above, top to bottom : 80. Walter Dorwin Teague : Shop Front    81. George Howe and William E. Lescaze : Drawing Room
Opposite : 82. Gilbert Rohde : Man's Study

the Museum's physical plant languished, attendance at the Museum in 1933 increased (per open days), as visitors sought inexpensive entertainment and were drawn by such Carnegie-funded exhibitions as *Contemporary Sculpture*, and by paintings from the Johnson Collection that had been installed by Marceau for the first time at the Museum in temporary galleries. When the federal government created the Civil Works Administration in November 1933, followed by the Works Progress (later Work Projects) Administration (WPA) in April 1935, Stokes and Kimball immediately submitted proposals for the completion of the Museum building (including galleries for modern art),[116] as well as improvements at Memorial Hall—all of which were granted. The Museum library was among the interiors studied (but never built) under these programs, Kimball remarking on the Howe-and-Lescaze-inspired design that "certain phases of the modern style are particularly well suited to the purposes of a library" (fig. 86).[117] The institution was the first, and over the course of the next seven and a half years, the largest museum recipient of WPA funds,[118] initially using the collections (referred to in the proposals as "antique materials") that were to be incorporated in the construction work to match, dollar for dollar, the government allotment, as required.[119] By November 1935, thanks to WPA funds that supplemented the diminished city appropriation, the Museum on Fairmount, Memorial Hall, and the Rodin Museum were again open seven days a week.[120]

In order to maintain or expand the Museum's programs in a period of general economic depression that was aggravated by a slender endowment and operating budget, Kimball had to find well-trained, devoted staff who would work hard for small pay. Accordingly, in the spring of 1934 he wrote Henry McIlhenny at Harvard: "Before you go away anywhere, & the sooner the better, I want to talk with you seriously about an appointment to the staff of the Museum."[121] Kimball's relationships with the McIlhennys had remained close after the death of Henry's father, John D. McIlhenny, who had served as the

Museum's president from 1918 until his death in 1925 and had bequeathed his art collection to the Museum.[122] Henry, meanwhile, was preparing to follow in his father's footsteps as a collector, hoping to become the kind of serious art professional his parents admired and to join the ranks of the important art historians, curators, and dealers to whom his parents had introduced him. In 1933 he wrote his mother from Harvard about a recent dinner party in Worcester, Massachusetts: "I felt in my element. Of course there was lots of gossip, the cynosure of all eyes being Lord Duveen who asked how you were and said he was shortly going to Philadelphia. . . . I met Gordon Washburn, head of the Buffalo Museum, who said that he had been at our house with Sachs. . . . Everybody, of course, gave me

advice as to what to do to be a perfect museum man."[123] Although McIlhenny's personal interests lay in French paintings—in 1930 he purchased Jean-Baptiste-Siméon Chardin's *Still Life with a Hare* (c. 1730), which he presented to the Museum in 1958, and with his mother the following year Henri de Toulouse-Lautrec's *At the Moulin Rouge: The Dance* (1890; bequeathed to the Museum at

Opposite : **86. Ludwig Babral** : proposed design for the Museum library interior on Fairmount : c. 1935 : Civil Works Administration Project
Above : **87.** Henri Gabriel Marceau : appointed assistant curator in 1926 : Museum director, 1955–64

his death)—Kimball needed the young man in what was then the unstaffed department of decorative arts. In 1934 McIlhenny (fig. 92) was named the Museum's assistant curator of decorative arts (at the time an unsalaried position), where he would remain for thirty years, until his retirement as curator in 1963.[124]

With the staff still much reduced (curatorial and administrative personnel had numbered over thirty persons in 1931–32, but only twelve in 1935–36),[125] McIlhenny joined Henry Clifford, recently promoted to associate curator of painting, and Henri Marceau (fig. 87), now the Museum's

assistant director as well as curator of painting and sculpture, to plan and produce the general program of exhibitions regardless of subject. In 1936, for example, McIlhenny was largely responsible for an important Degas exhibition ("the most comprehensive showing . . . ever attempted in America," according to Kimball)[126] to which he and Clifford lent works from their private collections and which McIlhenny's mother financed. In 1936–37 eleven new galleries were completed and opened under the first WPA grant, among them a series of French galleries and period rooms, for which Kimball gave McIlhenny credit. "The great inaugural installation of the

Above, left to right : **88. Maurice Marinot** : Vase : 1923 : acid-etched glass : H 7" : 1967-98-13 (cat. 112)   **89. Maurice Marinot** : Bottle : 1924 : acid-etched glass : H (bottle) 10" : 1967-98-16a,b (cat. 113)   **90. Maurice Marinot** : Bottle : 1923 : glass with encased enamel : H (bottle) 7 3/16" : 1967-98-10a,b (cat. 111)

French galleries is over, and we know what a success it was," Kimball wrote him, ". . . due above all to you."[127] At the same time Kimball expressed his appreciation more concretely by promoting McIlhenny from assistant to associate curator.

Over the long course of his curatorship and connection with the Museum, McIlhenny displayed little regard for modern and contemporary decorative arts. However, his mother and their cosmopolitan friends, among them Williamina and Rodolphe Meyer de Schauensee, began in the 1930s to purchase—for their homes in Philadelphia

and abroad—distinguished contemporary objects and tableware that were later given to the Museum. Frances McIlhenny acquired Lalique's masterful *Tourbillons* vase (fig. 95), its faceted edges painted with shiny black enamel, and other molded glasswares from the Lalique shop in Paris. The de Schauensees bought French glass by Lalique too, such as the *Margaret* vase (fig. 91), as well as Italian glass by Paolo Venini (fig. 126) and Gio Ponti's *Four Seasons* porcelain plates for Richard Ginori (fig. 93).[128] Other French glass of the period was subsequently added to the Museum's collections, most importantly, twenty pieces by Maurice Marinot, one of the most celebrated

Above : **91. René Lalique** : for Lalique, Paris : *Margaret* Vase : 1929 : patinated glass : H 9 1/8" : 1960-70-1 (cat. 105)

artist-glassmakers of the twentieth century (figs. 88–90, 129). In 1936 Louis V. Placé, Jr., vice president of W. V. McCahan Sugar Refining and Molasses Company in Philadelphia, gave the Museum a handsome silver dish designed and made by Georg Jensen (fig. 94).[129]

Museum president Stokes again made use of the *Bulletin* in February 1937, announcing a ten-year development campaign to raise $15.5 million, in part to fund the completion of the Museum's interior, permanent curatorial and administrative staff for care of the collections, and cataloguing and installation of additional works[130]—a

bold but necessary step during what Kimball described, at nearly the same time, as a period of "poverty and retrenchment."[131] The death of publisher Arthur H. Lea in 1938 brought the Museum a bequest of $50,000, as well as a collection of paintings, "conditioned upon the official designation . . . of said museum as 'Philadelphia Museum of Art,' its right and proper name."[132] The board readily acquiesced to the nomenclature, which was already in unofficial use, and the legal title of the Museum corporation was duly changed with little fanfare on April 15 of that year.[133]

Above : **92. Franklin Chenault Watkins** : *Portrait of Henry P. McIlhenny* : 1941 : oil on canvas : H 47" : 1986-26-38 (cat. 207)    Opposite : **93. Gio Ponti** : for Richard Ginori : *Inverno (Winter)* Plate from *Four Seasons* : c. 1923–30 : enameled porcelain : D 9" : 1990-102-1 (cat. 151)

Opposite : **94. Georg Jensen** : for Georg Jensen Sølvsmedie : Dish : 1919 : silver : D 14⁷/₁₆" : 1936-33-1 (cat. 93)    Above : **95. René Lalique** : for Lalique, Paris : *Tourbillons (Whirlwinds)* Vase : 1926 : enameled glass : H 8" : 1986-26-146 (cat. 104)

Shortly after *Organic Design* closed at the Museum, *Art in Advertising* opened, the second such exhibition held at the Museum and sponsored by the Art Directors Club of Philadelphia.[148] Museum president Stokes commented in a news release that, "while quite naturally one of the dominant notes of the show this year will be the vital role the artists of America are playing in the war effort, we believe the exhibition demonstrates convincingly a rapidly narrowing margin between the fine arts and the work of commercial artists whose works hitherto have been seen only in reproduction in the newspapers and magazines of the country and seldom in original on the walls of our important museums."[149] Kimball remarked on the addition of "a patriotic note" to the exhibition by a large group of war posters and "the handsome decoration with flags."[150]

Again, the Museum acquired nothing directly from *Art in Advertising*, but Jean Carlu's now well-known *America's Answer! Production* poster, which was featured in the exhibition, came to the Museum years later as a gift (fig. 103). Philadelphia graphic designer Matthew Leibowitz, formerly a student of Alexey Brodovitch at the Museum school, was also included in the exhibition (winning a prize for design and lettering in this, his first year of independent practice), and examples of his work were also eventually acquired by the Museum (fig. 104).

Following *Art in Advertising*, the Museum showed a group of modern French tapestries designed by Georges Braque, Raoul Dufy, Fernand Léger, Jean Lurçat, Henri Matisse, Joan Miró, and Georges Rouault. Commissioned

Above : **103. Jean Carlu** : for the U.S. Government Printing Office, Office for Emergency Management : *America's Answer! Production* Poster : 1942 : offset lithograph : H 29⁷/₈" : 2003-70-1 (cat. 27)   Opposite : **104. Matthew Leibowitz** : for Caedmon Records :  *H. L. Mencken: Speaking* Album Cover : 1958 : letterpress on Lustro Gloss paper : H 12¹/₂" : 2007-103-4 (cat. 108)

now appoint you regularly on the staff as assistant in Decorative Arts. . . . I know you understand, what we deeply regret, that we cannot compensate you for your services, but no doubt in good time promotion in rank and some honorarium will follow."[164]

There were additional staff, as well as board, changes at the Museum. Henry's mother, Frances McIlhenny, died during the war in 1943 and was replaced on the Museum board in 1948 by her daughter, Bonnie Wintersteen. John Story Jenks, chair of the museum committee for more than twenty years and credited by the board for building up the collections of Chinese art, his particular interest, died in 1946; and Museum president J. Stogdell Stokes died in 1947.[165] Sturgis Ingersoll, a committed collector of and advocate for modern art, in 1947 was named chair of the museum committee—at this time retitled the board of governors of the Museum—and the following year, president of the Museum (fig. 116). In a message to the Museum membership published in January 1948, Ingersoll wrote of his ambition "to create a focal point of inspiration and encouragement to the contemporary artist, since without contemporary art, the art of the past dies. In our great manufacturing city we must establish ideals of beautiful utility for the products of our looms and other manufactures [sic]."[166] Ingersoll saw Kimball bring three important modern art collections to the Museum: in 1943 that of Pennsylvania-born A. E. Gallatin (acquired permanently on Gallatin's death in 1952), a collection of largely geometric abstractions, including Léger's *The City* (1919) and Picasso's *Three Musicians* (1921); in 1949 photographs, paintings, and works on paper by the celebrated New York photographer and gallery owner Alfred Stieglitz;[167] and finally the collection of Louise and Walter Arensberg, which Kimball secured in 1949 but which came to the Museum only with the deaths of the Arensbergs in 1953 and 1954, respectively. The Arensbergs' gift included paintings by Georges Braque, Marcel Duchamp, and Francis Picabia as well as an outstanding group of sculptures by Constantin Brancusi and an

important collection of Pre-Columbian sculpture. Kimball had only recently ceded the field of Pre-Columbian art to the University Museum, but he made a necessary exception of the Arensberg gift.[168]

Kimball's skill in acquiring gifts of such magnitude was needed in the postwar years, as the Museum once again became dependent on city appropriations for capital projects, including completion of unassigned spaces and, in particular, construction of galleries to house the new collections of modern art. In 1947 an organization of professionals concerned with the fashion industry, known as the Fashion Group, assumed the task of securing financial support for the permanent installation and maintenance of galleries that would constitute a Fashion Wing, including in 1951 a contribution from one of its members for a twentieth-century fashion gallery that

Opposite : **115. June Groff** : Fabric (detail) : 1947 : screen-printed linen : W 54" : 1948-13-1 (cat. 78)   Above : **116.** R. Sturgis Ingersoll : Museum president, 1948–64

Opposite : **121.** Gallatin Collection : Philadelphia Museum of Art : 1954    Above : **122.** Arensberg Collection : Philadelphia Museum of Art : 1954

as "the culmination of Mr. Kimball's distinguished accomplishment."[179] In one of his last letters, Kimball seemed to agree with that assessment, writing Marceau from Florence: "My first reaction, in the great Botticelli room [of the Uffizi], was how right Sturgis is in saying we can never buck the European museums. . . . All this is why we have a chance, scooping everyone but Basel on the 20th century."[180] It would take another half-century before the design collections could share in the Museum's modernist reputation. Kimball died in Munich in August 1955. A memorial tribute, written by Horace Jayne and Henri Marceau, stressed not only his heroic accomplishment in "making a museum out of a mole hill,"[181] but that he remained (like Edwin Atlee Barber) a publishing scholar of great distinction until his death.[182]

Marceau was a trained architect, like Kimball, and had been closely involved with the completion of the Museum's interior spaces, while remaining chief of the division of painting and sculpture and curator of the Johnson Collection. Continuing Kimball's building program throughout his tenure as director, Marceau began in the Museum's south wing with the installation of the Japanese temple, Japanese tea house and garden, Chinese temple, and Chinese scholar's study, all acquired decades earlier. He also oversaw completion of the Great Stair Hall, the auditorium underneath it, and an area at the head of the stairs reserved for the arms and armor collection of Otto von Kienbusch, secured by Kimball in 1951–52 and bequeathed to the Museum by Kienbusch in 1977.

Curator Henry McIlhenny, long encouraged by the board to organize a major exhibition,[183] chose to concentrate his later career on eighteenth- and nineteenth-century Philadelphia subjects, with shows in 1952–53 on the furniture makers Henry Connelly and Ephraim Haines, in 1956 on Philadelphia silver (assisted by board of governors member and collector Walter Jeffords), and in 1957 on Tucker porcelain, as well as an exhibition on Shaker arts and crafts in 1962.[184] McIlhenny also was responsible for the installation of a wing

of American decorative arts, which opened in November 1958 and included American and European silver, eighteenth-century Philadelphia furniture, and the arts of rural Pennsylvania. In his last annual departmental report before retiring at the end of 1963, he made clear the collecting priorities he had pursued: "It has long been the policy of the Department that Philadelphiana must be given especial attention, and the retiring curators have long felt that Philadelphia furniture, silver and other works of art of local origin must be acquired, even to the neglect of European objects that sorely tempted their acquisitive desires."[185]

The years 1963 and 1964 represented a watershed period in the history of the Museum's staffing.[186] Not only did McIlhenny retire as curator of decorative arts after a thirty-year tenure—"his enduring monument," noted Ingersoll, "is our Collection of Decorative Arts and its installation"[187]— but Louis C. Madeira, the department's associate curator, retired as well; McIlhenny was then elected to the board of trustees, and Madeira to the board of governors. Most notably, Henri Marceau asked to be retired as director; cited by the Museum as "Fiske Kimball's right arm" and successor, he "had endeared himself to multitudes, from charwomen to mayors . . . [and] played an important role in substantially every artistic activity in his adopted city of Philadelphia."[188]

While the administration of the Museum underwent major changes, the committee structure of the board was reorganized in 1964. Sturgis Ingersoll retired as president of the Museum to serve as chair of the board of trustees, and his place as principal officer of the corporation and board was taken by Bonnie Wintersteen. The corporation's bylaws were amended to include standing committees focused on specific executive and administrative concerns as well as curatorial areas. According to the bylaws of 1964–65, new curatorial departmental committees, including a committee for decorative arts, would function in an advisory capacity to the president and director with respect to the Museum's programs and projects pertaining to their

123. **Marcel Breuer** : Desk and Chair for Bryn Mawr College : 1938 : maple plywood : L (desk) 50" : H (chair) 33 1/2" : 1999-11-1–3 (cat. 24)

Opposite : 137. The Museum's Great Stair Hall "wrapped" by the artist Christo : 1970   Above : 138. A celebration of Christo's installation at the Museum

149

**Product Environment: New Furniture** arrived at the Museum at the end of September 1970 from the City Art Museum of Saint Louis (now known as the Saint Louis Art Museum), displaying the kind of innovative domestic furnishings favored by Hathaway and Inter-Society members. In connection with the exhibition, New York manufacturing firm Habitat gave the Museum a group of polished aluminum and steel objects in undecorated geometric shapes by the firm's president, industrial designer Paul Mayen (fig. 141). Setting a precedent for acquiring contemporary designs related to exhibitions, *Product Environment* also met Turner's goal of introducing new work to Philadelphians. "'Product Environment' is off— and from all evidence it is off to a flying start," he wrote to Bartine Stoner at the advertising firm of N. W. Ayer and Son. "It is one of those rare exhibitions that not only delights visitors but seems to attract families in considerable numbers, the happiest sort of exhibition for this Museum."[27]

**Product Environment : New Furniture : 1970**

Opposite and above : **139 and 140.** Gallery views
Inset, right : **141. Paul Mayen** : for Habitat : Sand Urn and Waste Receptacle : c. 1965 : Trexiloy : H 25³/₁₆" : 1970-206-3 (cat. 123)

of trustees that since the Museum functioned in a world where an increasing number of young people were interested in their environment, the Museum should take the lead in improving the aesthetic quality of their lives.[28] In late 1971 the department of urban outreach commissioned from Washington, D.C. artist Gene Davis a monumental stripe painting (of traffic paint and fast-drying, durable, high-gloss enamel) titled *Franklin's Footpath*, in front of the Museum on the asphalt surface of the Benjamin Franklin Parkway. Hailed as the largest painting in the world—it was the size of a football field—the work was executed by staff artists from the department of urban outreach and high school students in an extraordinary community effort using street-painting equipment lent by the city (fig. 142).

At the same time, the Museum began preparations for the coinciding celebrations of the nation's bicentennial and the Museum's centennial in 1976. Philadelphia would be an obvious center of the national celebration, and Museum staff were charged by the board to organize a major exhibition of American art. Led by pharmaceutical manufacturer and Museum trustee Robert L. McNeil, Jr., the board in 1969 had previously created a new committee for American art, with responsibility for the Museum's strong collections of American paintings, sculptures, and decorative arts;[29] however, it was only with the appointment in 1973 of a curator, Darrel Sewell, that the committee acquired a department.[30] Building on the important collections acquired by Fiske Kimball, a new department of twentieth-century art was also established for that area in 1972; its curator of painting, Anne d'Harnoncourt, later the Museum's director, returned to the Museum from the Art Institute of Chicago to fill the post.[31]

Henry McIlhenny had originally opposed the creation of a department of contemporary art, arguing to the executive committee that the painting and sculpture committee, which he headed, should not be divided: "This Museum aims to represent the history of art, starting with Christ. If

Opposite : **146. Wendell Castle** : *Molar* Chair : 1973 : fiberglass-reinforced polyester : H 26" : 1973-99-1 (cat. 30)    Above : **147. Gio Ponti** : for Ideal
Standard : Toilet : 1953 : porcelain : H 15¹/₈" : 1983-52-2 (cat. 152)

# A SERIES OF
# DESIGN EXHIBITIONS

**I**n early 1973 architect Richard Saul Wurman joined the Inter-Society; he would later become internationally known as a pioneer of "information architecture" as well as creator of the popular *Access* guidebooks. Wurman developed a number of strategies that have since guided the growth of the Museum's design collections, particularly his insistence on the need to contact manufacturers directly when trying to acquire objects by donation.[43] He also assumed responsibility for investigating themes that could shape Collab '74. With Helen Drutt and architect and Inter-Society chair Roland Gallimore, Wurman proposed sponsoring an international-design trade fair to present each country's leading products, although it soon became apparent that instead of inviting many countries at once, it would be more practical (and economical) to feature a single country each year. Thus the exhibition of crafts and industrial objects *British Contemporary Design*[44] was conceived for Collab '74, and it fell to the department of European decorative arts after 1700 to realize what became the first in a long series of design exhibitions produced for the committee and the Museum.

Britain represented a well-calculated theme for the initial exhibition because the Design Council of Great Britain and the Duke of Edinburgh, through their respective programs of national design awards granted to industry, could provide a ready-made short list of exhibition objects from which to select. In addition, the Crafts Advisory Committee of Great Britain helped us to identify handcrafted objects and to contact the country's most prominent craftspersons for their recent, best work. As we discovered, British manufacturers not only wanted to lend their award-winning pieces, but also to donate them to the Museum.

In order to cover the exhibition expenses (Evan Turner had made it clear that the Museum had no space in its own budget to finance the show),[45] and guided by the Museum's development office, the Inter-Society launched a fund-raising campaign that netted not only contributions but also a new audience. Ninety percent of the individuals and design-trade firms that helped support the exhibition had no prior history of contribution to the Museum or Museum-sponsored events.[46] This was an important moment for the Museum and the Inter-Society, as it revealed that modern and contemporary design had its own audience.

*British Contemporary Design*, a small, elegant exhibition, was designed and installed by Inter-Society members in collaboration with Museum staff. It consisted of thirty-six manufactured objects lent by British firms, thirty-two handmade objects lent by the Crafts Advisory Committee, and eleven objects lent to the exhibition from private collections and the Museum, all displayed on white modular platforms banded in red and framed by walls painted deep blue (fig. 148). Three hundred guests attended the subscription opening of the exhibition, where Sir Peter Shepheard, dean of the Graduate School of Fine Arts at the University of Pennsylvania and member of the Duke of Edinburgh's prize committee in 1971 and 1972, delivered a lecture. The exhibition and opening event accomplished the Inter-Society's core mission of adding works to the collection—twenty-nine in all—and generating substantial new support for and interest in the Museum's collections of modern and contemporary design.

**British Contemporary Design : 1974**

Opposite : 148. Gallery view : 1974    Above : 149. Gerald Abramovitz : for Best & Lloyd : *Cantilever* Desk Lamp : 1961 : aluminum, steel : H 20" : 1974-58-1 (cat. 4)

Among the gifts to the Museum from *British Contemporary Design* were the *Apollo 1225* armchair designed by Robert Heritage for use aboard HMS Queen Elizabeth II; Robin Day's polypropylene stacking chair, arguably the first to be designed in that material (fig. 151); David Powell's semidisposable ABS-plastic flatware; printed textiles designed by Shirley Craven and Peter McCulloch (figs. 150, 152); and Gerald Abramovitz's *Cantilever* desk lamp (fig. 149). The American Institute of Interior Design supported the Museum's acquisition of handcrafted works by artists who included Peter Collingwood, Hans Coper, and Lucie Rie (figs. 153–55).

**British Contemporary Design : 1974**

Opposite : 150. **Shirley Craven** : for Hull Traders : *Five Fabric* (detail) : 1967 : screen-printed linen and cotton : W 50" : 1975-8-1a–c (cat. 40)

Above : 151. **Robin Day** : for Hille : *Polyprop* Stacking Chair : 1963 : steel, polypropylene : H 29$^{3}/_{4}$" : 1974-150-1 (cat. 43)

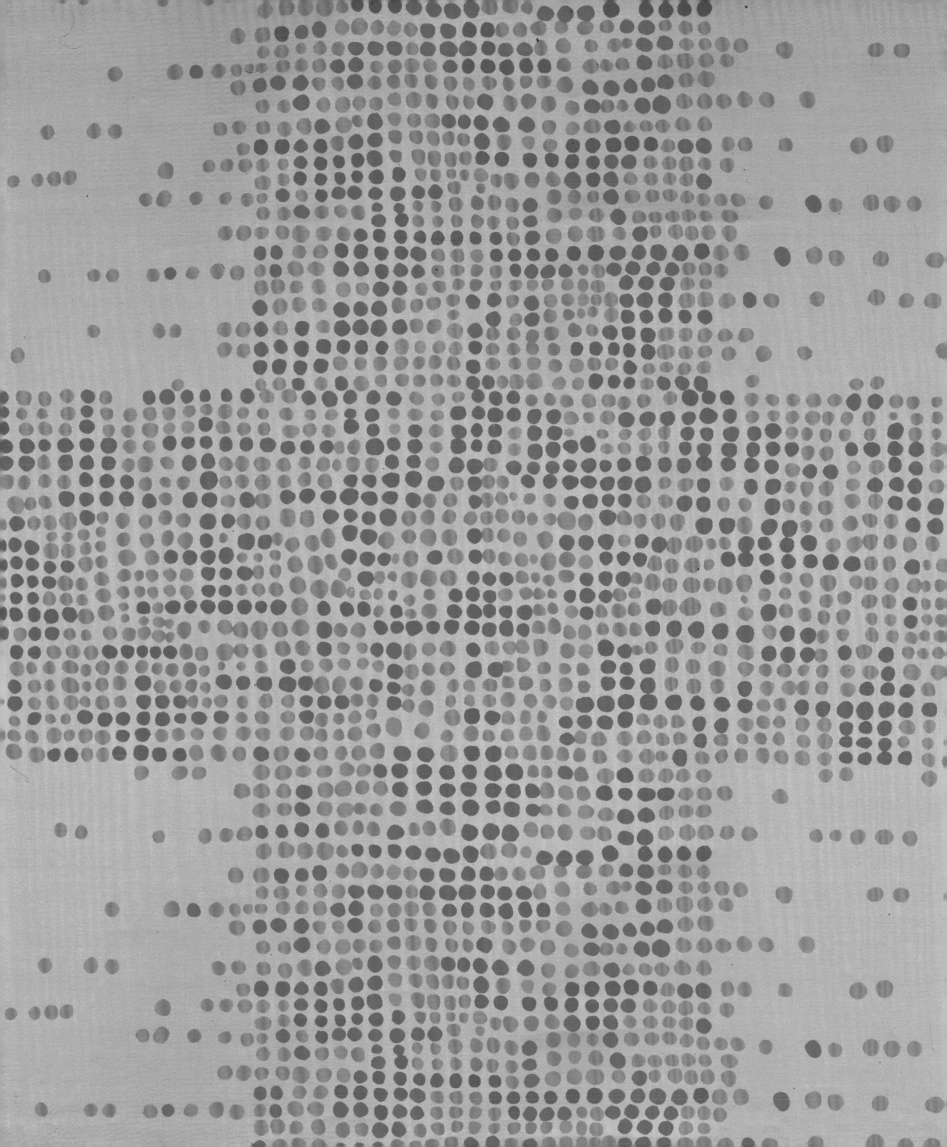

**British Contemporary Design : 1974**

Opposite : **152. Peter McCulloch** : for Hull Traders : *Cruachan* Fabric (detail) : 1963 : screen-printed cotton : W 48" : 1975-8-2a,b (cat. 126)
Above, left to right : **153. Lucie Rie** : Bottle : 1974 : glazed porcelain : H 11" : 1975-46-6 (cat. 158)    **154. Hans Coper** : Vase : 1974 : stoneware : H 9 1/8" :
1975-46-3 (cat. 39)    **155. Hans Coper** : Vase : 1974 : stoneware : H 7 3/4" : 1975-46-2 (cat. 38)

Just days after the opening of *British Contemporary Design*, another, smaller design exhibition was installed. Organized by the Women's Committee of the Museum, *A Touch of Gold*[47] displayed handcrafted contemporary jewelry, chiefly by Philadelphia artists, to celebrate the tenth anniversary of the Museum's Art Sales and Rental Gallery, a small gallery within the Museum that featured orginal crafts and works of art for sale. The works on view were available for purchase, and the exhibition thus forecast the much larger and more diverse Philadelphia Craft Show that the Women's Committee would initiate three years later. Both exhibition projects were modest of necessity, as they took place during the installation of the Museum's air-conditioning system. In fact, the two shows were shoehorned into an almost overwhelming schedule of construction and activity as the Museum prepared for its own centennial and the nation's bicentennial celebrations in 1976.

Under Turner's direction and the leadership of trustee Lewine Russell, indomitable chair of the Museum's building committee, so many significant construction projects were accomplished between 1969 and 1978 (when Russell resigned as chair)—notably climate control for the entire building, new special-exhibition galleries, and the creation of the new American wing—that the trustees jubilantly acknowledged: "The fifty year process of finishing the interior of the Museum building has been virtually completed and the Museum faces its second fifty years with a building which for the first time is properly equipped to function as a modern museum facility."[48] Even as the Museum's interior was being concluded, however, the board was already seriously considering the purchase of the former Fidelity Mutual Life Insurance building opposite the Museum at Fairmount and Pennsylvania avenues,[49] to provide space for its ever increasing collections and programs. This prospect would become a reality in 1999 when the support of the city of Philadelphia and Ruth and Raymond G. Perelman, the latter then chair of the Museum's board of trustees, made it possible for the institution to acquire the landmark building.

The many improvements made to the Museum could be carried out only by closing the building to the public from April 1975 through February 1976, while the staff moved and ultimately reinstalled nearly every one of some 450,000 objects in renovated galleries or new storage areas. With the help of my colleague Suzanne F. Wells, our department moved thousands of ceramics, including modern and contemporary works, to a new study-storage space, piece by piece in padded carts; we also inventoried, planned, and supervised the transfer of the Museum's furniture collection to its new storage areas. Following *British Contemporary Design*, Collab had envisioned a series of exhibitions that would explore design by country of origin, but other departmental concerns took priority, including the United States bicentennial exhibition *Philadelphia: Three Centuries of American Art*;[50] the Museum's centennial anniversary celebration; and development of a major international exhibition, *The Second Empire: Art in France under Napoleon III*.[51] Organized with my colleague Joseph J. Rishel, the Museum's curator of European paintings before 1900, and a team of French curators, *The Second Empire* opened in October 1978, before traveling to Detroit and then Paris, and occupied all 13,000 square feet of the Museum's new special exhibition galleries. It was described in the *New York Times* as "the single most outstanding exhibition of the year,"[52] representing "a

major challenge to established artistic opinion,"[53] an assessment shared by the *Washington Post*: "deliciously subversive . . . it pokes a hundred holes in that agreed-on fable called The Origin of Modern Art."[54] A number of the decorative arts objects arrived in Philadelphia from France in need of treatment, and in 1979, for the first time in the Museum's history, an objects conservator was added to the staff: P. Andrew Lins would eventually take responsibility for the conservation, preservation, and treatment of all the Museum's collections of decorative arts and sculpture.[55] However, throughout the project modern design remained on my mind, and during a research trip to Paris, I found an elegant French Art Deco writing desk made by Jacques-Émile Ruhlmann. Collab subsequently purchased the desk as a gift to honor the Museum's centennial (fig. 280), and in 1977 it was displayed at the Museum in *Gifts to Mark a Century: An Exhibition Celebrating the Centennial of the Philadelphia Museum of Art.*[56]

During the 1970s the heavy demand placed on the Museum's staff and interior spaces—by the construction of an air-conditioning system, the bicentennial exhibition, and the installation and reinstallation of the American wing as well as other permanent galleries—made it virtually impossible for Collab to plan fund-raising projects within the Museum building. Collab '75, a public auction of modern and contemporary designs, was thus held in Memorial Hall, the first of a long series of fund-raising auctions that took place at different locations and finally at the Museum. Under the remarkably efficient direction of chair and interior designer Elisabeth Fraser, friends and business associates of Collab members (including manufacturers and their sales representatives) donated some 140 contemporary manufactured and handcrafted objects, a model followed at succeeding auctions. George Freeman, of the Philadelphia auctioneers Samuel T. Freeman and Company, advised the group on charity-auction procedures and served as auctioneer to some 500 guests. The proceeds of the Collab '75 and Collab '76 auctions were used to purchase the Ruhlmann writing desk,

the group's most expensive acquisition to date. From the 1975 auction an executive lounge chair and ottoman designed by Charles Eames was purchased with funds contributed by Mr. and Mrs. Adolph G. Rosengarten, Jr., in memory of Calvin S. Hathaway, who had died in 1974. Through Helen Drutt, Collab was also able to sponsor the acquisition of additional fine contemporary crafts for the collections, including a raku-glazed earthenware vessel by Wayne Higby (fig. 156) and an Indonesian boxwood bowl carved by Robert Stocksdale (fig. 157).

When the newly reinstalled and air-conditioned Museum reopened in February 1976, modern and contemporary design was given its own small gallery within the section of the building devoted to modern art, fulfilling Turner's earlier promise to Collab. Our display of Marinot glass, Scandinavian ceramics, and a Puiforcat tureen, juxtaposed with Amédée Ozenfant's similarly composed still-life painting *Nacres No. 2* (1923–26), was a particular favorite with the press. The *New York Times* celebrated the Museum's reopening as a great victory over the challenges posed by the monumental building: "The museum is already bursting with new energy and sparkling with a combination of face-lifting and genuine rejuvenation. . . . a worthy habitation for its great collections."[57] Museum president George Cheston described the reopening as "one of the most exciting and personally satisfying events" during his tenure of eight years and gave fulsome credit to Turner for achieving it.[58]

Opposite : **156. Wayne Higby** : *Many Rocks Pass* : 1976 : glazed and unglazed earthenware : H 12" : 1976-106-1 (cat. 82)
Above : **157. Robert Stocksdale** : Bowl : 1975 : Indonesian boxwood : D 8 1/4" : 1976-107-1 (cat. 184)

The Museum staff was therefore taken by complete surprise when only a year later Turner announced his resignation as director, just after the inauguration of the new American wing in April 1977. In his letter of resignation Turner acknowledged that the Museum was "at a major turning point in its history," and noted his "great satisfaction" in the "realization of our programs leading up to the Centennial." However, he concluded, "it is proper that someone else should undertake the challenges of the Directorship and bring different energies to bear as the Museum faces its second century."[59] Turner's resignation was accepted with regret by William P. Wood, the Harvard-trained lawyer and collector of Indian paintings who in 1976 had succeeded George Cheston as Museum president. Wood further recognized the "magnitude of

Dr. Turner's contribution" to the Museum's board of trustees and cited a long list of his accomplishments.[60] Comparing Turner to "the cowboy hero who rides off into the sunset after he's cleaned up the town," the Christian Science Monitor cited the Museum's "massive renovation and reinstallation . . . ushering the museum into the twentieth-century."[61] In his last annual report as director, Turner summarized what he felt were the most important achievements of his directorship, among them developing a professional Museum staff, creating order in the collections with new galleries and study-storage areas, and making the Museum more accessible to the public through the activities of the division of education and department of urban outreach. Collab chair Elisabeth Fraser expressed the group's appreciation for Turner, "its staunchest

personnel—including guards, art handlers, the individual responsible for packing and shipping art, and craft technicians such as carpenters, painters, and plasterers. The city's bleak financial outlook reflected the effects of a global recession and inflation triggered in 1973 by the oil embargo and subsequent energy crisis. In the winter of 1977 the Museum took its own steps to address the energy crisis by closing the Fairmount Park Houses and the Rodin Museum, and by turning off lights and hot water at night in the building on Fairmount. Heated by steam rather than gas, the Museum remained open during regular visitor hours, although a number of galleries were closed for lack of guards; in addition, the Museum was forced temporarily to discontinue programs such as studio art classes and to cut public services, among them visitors' use of the library and slide library.

There were no funds for acquisitions in fiscal 1977, but among other gifts the Museum received a lamp and six pieces of twentieth-century furniture from Atelier International—constituting the most substantial gift from a manufacturer in many years—including lighting and furniture by Tobia and Afra Scarpa (fig. 158), Achille and Pier Giacomo Castiglioni (fig. 159), and Vico Magistretti. A small exhibition of these and other pieces was organized in the Director's Corridor of the Museum during the spring of 1979 by Suzanne Wells, soon to be named assistant curator, who also published an exhibition checklist that was distributed without charge in the gallery. Against the background of preparations for the Museum's *Second Empire* exhibition, Collab presented its annual fundraising auction in 1977 at the Marketplace Design Center, and in 1978 at the Academy of Music Rehearsal Hall, both in Philadelphia. In memory of Roland Gallimore, architect and former Collab chair who had died recently, Collab used the proceeds from Collab '78 to support the Museum's purchase of a tubular-steel and cane chair and stool designed by Mies van der Rohe (fig. 85). This gift inaugurated a tradition of donating objects in honor of Collab chairs that has continued to the present.

supporter . . . through [whose] efforts Collab has been able to reach its capabilities."[62] To find a successor to Evan Turner, the board appointed a search committee,[63] on which I served as staff representative along with Arnold Jolles, who since 1974 had been the Museum's assistant director for art and would serve as acting director in the interim.

Despite the Museum's impressive achievements under the direction of Turner, and the city of Philadelphia's major contributions to the Museum's capital budget for air-conditioning, renovation, and construction, the institution faced tremendous pressures due to eroding financial support from the city for other services. Of particular importance was the gradual depletion of municipal

158. Tobia Scarpa and Afra Scarpa : for Atelier International and Cassina : *Soriana* Lounge Chair and Ottoman : 1970 : chromed metal, polyurethane, Dacron, leather : H (chair) 27" : H (ottoman) 15 3/4" : 1978-21-1a,b (cat. 172)

In July 1978 the Museum's nominating and search committees unanimously recommended fifty-six-year-old Jean Sutherland Boggs, then professor of fine arts at Harvard—where she had received A.M. and Ph.D. degrees in art history from Radcliffe College—as director, to assume her duties in March 1979 (fig. 160). Boggs was the first woman director of the Philadelphia Museum of Art and, as such, the first to direct one of the country's largest museums, a fact little remarked by the Museum's trustees in the face of her formidable accomplishments as a scholar, an educator, and a museum director.[64] Boggs's aesthetic interests extended well beyond her chosen field of modern painting. In a typescript preserved in the Museum's archives, Boggs, who grew up in Canada, described her first visit to the Museum of Modern Art in New York in 1939, at the age of seventeen, to see an exhibition of Italian works that had been on view at the San Francisco World's Fair: "For the first time in my life I saw, pristinely installed, Botticelli's *Birth of Venus*, Verrocchio's *David*, Titian's *Paul III*. A taste for the old within the new was born within me. I enjoyed feeling that the predictable inhabitants of the Museum of Modern Art essentially belonged with Botticelli's *Venus*."[65]

Boggs's broad interests led her to support Collab's goals and programs. She proposed, for example, that the group sponsor a lecture by Isamu Noguchi and help develop a small, auxiliary exhibition of his commercial designs to accompany the major exhibition *Noguchi's Imaginary Landscapes*, which would open at the Museum in October 1979.[66] As a result, a group of Noguchi's mulberry-bark-paper *Akari* lamps was shown in conjunction with the exhibition and given to the Museum by the artist (fig. 161). Noguchi's lecture for Collab filled the Museum's auditorium and "enchanted everyone."[67] Collab '79, an auction held that September (once again at the Marketplace), was as successful as its predecessors. In the following two years Collab again sponsored auctions, as well as illustrated lectures in 1980 by Mies van der Rohe's daughter, Georgia van der Rohe (who presented a film about her father), and in 1981 by architect Michael Graves. Boggs wrote me to

say how successful she thought the last auction had been: "I do hope you thoroughly enjoy the fruits of the endeavor—major new acquisitions for the collection."[68] In fact, the proceeds made possible the purchase of an important silver cup by Josef Hoffmann (fig. 310),[69] and a chair designed by Peter Behrens presented in honor of Collab chair Elisabeth Fraser. Building on Hathaway's earlier acquisition of the collection of Thonet chairs, the Museum thus began to assemble a core group of objects representing the important turn-of-the-century modern reform styles of Secession and Jugendstil, to which it would continue to add works in the years to come. At the end of 1981 Boggs wrote to Collab: "We cannot thank you enough for all you are doing. . . . You have been very busy and very generous."[70]

Opposite : 159. Achille Castiglioni and Pier Giacomo Castiglioni : for Flos : *Taccia* Table Lamp : 1962 : aluminum, glass : H 21" : 1977-199-1 (cat. 29)
Above : 160. Jean Sutherland Boggs : Museum director, 1979–82

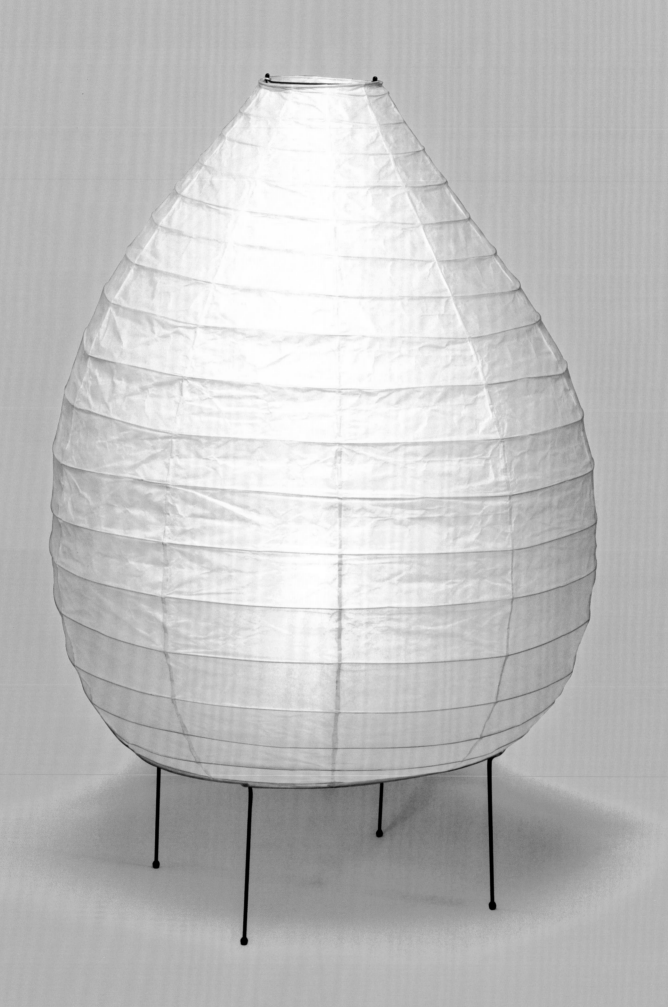

Opposite : **161. Isamu Noguchi** : for George Kovacs : *Akari* Floor Lamp : 1975 : mulberry-bark paper, bamboo, metal : H 45" : 1979-87-1a–d (cat. 139)
Above : **162. Isamu Noguchi** : for Knoll : Table Lamp : 1948 : plastic, wood : H 15³/₄" : 1977-85-1 (cat. 138)

In early 1979 I began discussing with Collab the organization of a major exhibition of modern and contemporary design. It was difficult to define the scope of the project, but with the encouragement of Collab chair Hava Gelblum and others it was concluded that material postdating World War II offered the most exciting and novel possibilities for exhibition, with a focus on objects of aesthetic distinction that were innovative in their forms, manufacturing techniques, and materials. Envisioned as a kind of sequel to the Museum's 1932 exhibition *Design for the Machine*, the show would include some four hundred objects made for household use, from appliances to armchairs, reflecting changing tastes, lifestyles, and technology. By 1980 I had prepared a tentative exhibition list and begun to contact manufacturers for help in assembling *Design Since 1945*, the first comprehensive survey in this country of recent decorative arts and designs. Over the next three years funding for the exhibition and its accompanying publication was provided not only by Collab, but by grants from corporations and public and private foundations.

*Design Since 1945* was on view at the Museum from October 1983 to January 1984.[71] George Nelson (fig. 164) designed the exhibition to allow controlled circulation among various groups of objects that were generally arranged by medium and in chronological order (figs. 165–71, 173–96). Throughout, video programs, didactic labels, and objects from the larger world of design helped to acquaint visitors with manufacturing processes and the effects of technology on style and products. Seven "designer profiles"—of Charles Eames, Arne Jacobsen, George Nelson himself, Dieter Rams, Ettore Sottsass, Tapio Wirkkala, and Marco Zanuso—consisting of photographs, objects, chronologies, and quotations, underscored the impact of creative individuals on the field and conveyed a sense of their personal style, achievements, and attitudes toward design as a whole. A section devoted to ergonomics invited visitors to test various examples of office chairs, and included a video program in which Niels Diffrient discussed his own ergonomically designed chair.

To introduce discussions of molding and miniaturization, a fiberglass Corvette shell was suspended over a group of molded plastic furniture, while Explorer 1 and other communication satellites (borrowed from the National Air and Space Museum in Washington, D.C.) hung above the appliances section. The exhibition included a number of audiovisual programs. Period commercials were shown on Philco Predicta (1958) and Sony Profeel (1979) televisions, marking the wide distance in taste, lifestyle, and technology within two decades of design.

A continuous, two-hour program took place in a small theater, screening short videos on individual designers. Nelson was circumspect on the subject of the audiovisual programs: "I am fearful of any 20-minute show on the main path through the exhibit," he wrote. "Bottlenecks for sure. . . . It should be possible to show the range of Eames's activities in 2–3 minutes. After all, the standard TV commercial is 30 seconds, and some of them seem interminable!"[72] A 251-page, fully illustrated catalogue provided the theoretical basis for the exhibition and

included the essays of sociologist Herbert Gans and sixteen internationally known designers and manufacturers who had helped shape the history they described, along with biographies and bibliographies of the designers and manufacturers (fig. 163).[73]

Like *Design for the Machine* a half-century earlier, the exhibition attracted a remarkable amount of press coverage. The *New York Times* called the show "brilliant" and named the catalogue "the design reference handbook of the decade."[74] This critical acclaim was reaffirmed by the *Washington Post*, the *Christian Science Monitor*, the *Boston Globe*, *Time* magazine, scholarly journals such as the *New Criterion*, and foreign publications, including *Svenska Dagbladet*, Sweden's largest daily newspaper, and the *Sunday Press* of London.[75]

Jean Boggs believed that it was important for programmatic activities to be developed around special exhibitions, in order to strengthen their impact and reach larger audiences.

Accordingly, a wide range of programs was organized: Philadelphia's first intercollegiate design course, taught at the Museum cooperatively by faculty members from Drexel University, Moore College of Art, Philadelphia College of Art, and Philadelphia College of Textiles and Science; "Objects and Objectives," a symposium featuring six internationally recognized designers and theorists— among them, Nicholas Negroponte, founder of the Media Lab at the Massachusetts Institute of Technology, who talked about the future of human-computer interaction; a lecture series that included presentations by NASA astronaut James Bagian and consumer advocate Ralph Nader; and a panel discussion, supported by Collab and the Friends of the Museum, with architects Charles Gwathmey and Robert Stern and other designers on the influence of product design on contemporary interiors.

By the time the exhibition and these programs took place, however, Boggs was no longer director of the Museum, having been asked in 1982 by the Canadian government to head a specially designated Crown Corporation that would supervise the design and construction of two new national museums and recommend architects and sites for them.[76] Before she left the Philadelphia Museum of Art, however, Boggs initiated an extensive study of programming and planning to evaluate the uses and shortages of space within the Museum building, and asked Collab to suggest architects who might carry out the project.[77] Led by architect and trustee James Nelson Kise, the Museum's building committee interviewed ten Philadelphia firms. In February 1980 the firm of Venturi, Rauch and Scott Brown was appointed to conduct the architectural study; a year later the firm addressed the board with its plan and goals, which included improving public perception of the collections and their relationship to the spatial sequence of the Museum, particularly with regard to the Johnson Collection. Integrating the Johnson Collection and other galleries containing European art, reinstalling the Museum's European collections, and renovating the galleries of modern and contemporary art were among

Design Since 1945 : 1983–84

Opposite : 163. Exhibition catalogue : edited by Kathryn B. Hiesinger and George H. Marcus (Philadelphia: Philadelphia Museum of Art, 1983)
Above : 164. Designer George Nelson and Kathryn Hiesinger amid construction for the exhibition

**Ergonomics:** The study of the human being in relation to the objects and tools he uses, the engineering of equipment for efficient use.

**Please be seated!**

**Design Since 1945 : 1983–84**
165 and 166. Gallery views

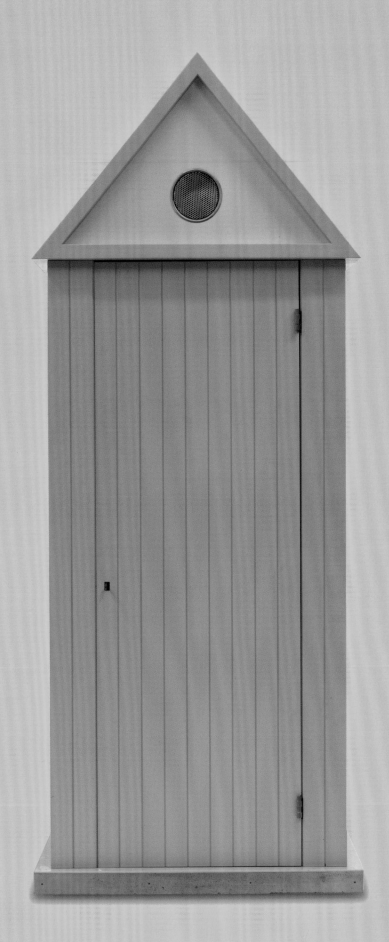

**Design Since 1945 : 1983–84**

Opposite : **174. Nathalie du Pasquier** : for Rainbow : *Gabon* Fabric (detail) : 1982 : screen-printed cotton : W 60" : 1983-119-1 (cat. 143)
Above : **175. Aldo Rossi** : for Molteni : *Cabina dell'Elba* Wardrobe : 1980 : particle board, plastic laminate, brass : H 7' 6¹/₄" : 2000-70-2 (cat. 163)

The works of contemporary design acquired from *Design Since 1945* included a number of pieces from the Italian postmodern design collective Memphis, which had been founded in the winter of 1980–81 proclaiming the aesthetic and metaphysical values of color, symbol, ornamented surfaces, heterogeneous materials, and irregular shapes. Manufacturer Abet Laminati gave the Museum three works by Memphis founder Ettore Sottsass, his *Nefertiti* desk (fig. 197) and *Superbox* cupboard and, with additional support from Collab, his signature *Casablanca* sideboard (fig. 173), along with Javier Errando Mariscal's *Hilton* trolley, also made for Memphis (fig. 177). The Philadelphia Museum of Art was the first museum in the country to own and exhibit most of these works, and to show the works of Mariscal, who traveled from Spain to attend the opening (and was later to design the logo for the 1992 Barcelona Olympics). The Spanish textile firm of Marieta gave the Museum some of Mariscal's printed fabrics for the exhibition (figs. 176, 185), and B. D. Ediciones de Diseño presented his *Duplex* stool (fig. 183), designed for a bar in Barcelona. Carlos Riart, also from Barcelona, donated his golden-hooved *Desnuda* chair (fig. 184). Other Memphis pieces in the exhibition included Marco Zanini's *Alpha Centauri* vase (fig. 180) and Nathalie du Pasquier's *Gabon* fabric (fig. 174); both were gifts of the New York firm Furniture of the 20th-Century. Building on the collection's strength in this area, gifts of Italian postmodern material continued to arrive throughout the following decade, among them Matteo Thun's *Nefertiti* tea service (fig. 308) and Aldo Rossi's wardrobe inspired by European beach cabanas (fig. 175). Recognizing that the exhibition had not done justice to Italian theorist and designer Alessandro Mendini, in 2000 I was pleased to have the opportunity to purchase his hand-painted Proust armchair (fig. 198).

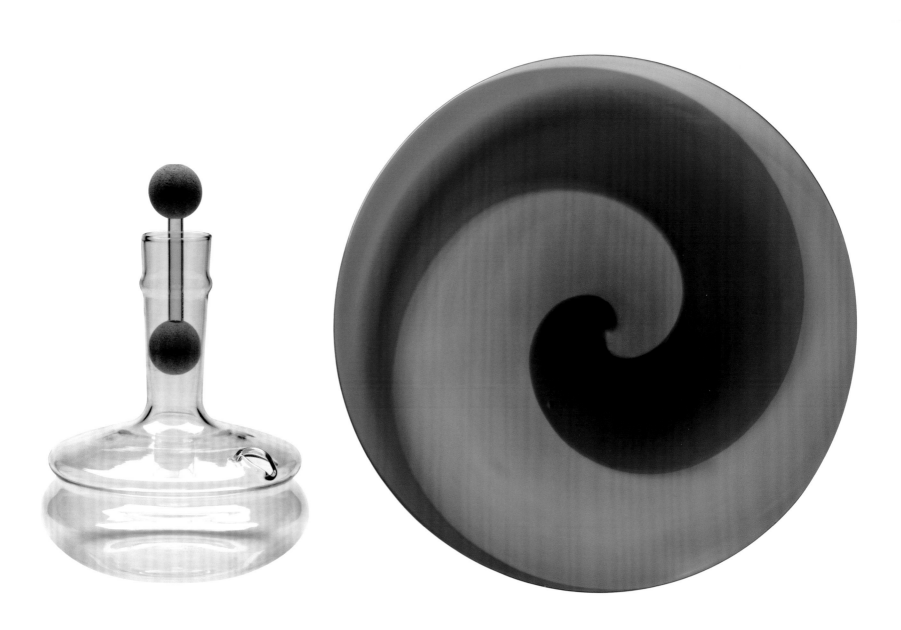

**Design Since 1945 : 1983–84**

Opposite and above, left to right : **178.** Kaj Franck : for Nuutajärvi : *Kremlin Bells* Double Decanter : 1957 : glass : H 13³/4" : 1982-33-1a–c (cat. 60)
**179.** Tapio Wirkkala : for Venini : *Bolla* Vase : 1970 : glass : H 13³/8" : 1983-151-4 (cat. 214)    **180.** Marco Zanini : for Toso and Memphis :
*Alpha Centauri* Vase : 1982 : glass : H 15⁵/8" : 1983-112-5 (cat. 222)    **181.** Peter Schlumbohm : for Chemex : Water Kettle : 1949 : Pyrex glass, cork :
H 12⁵/₁₆" : 1983-4-2a,b (cat. 173)    **182.** Tapio Wirkkala : for Venini : *Coreano* Dish : 1970 : glass : D 15³/4" : 1983-151-3 (cat. 213)

**Design Since 1945 : 1983–84**

Above, left to right : **183.** Javier Errando Mariscal : for B. D. Ediciones de Diseño : *Duplex* Stool : 1981 : metal, leather : H 32¹⁄₂" : 1983-44-1 (cat. 118)
**184. Carlos Riart** : for Temco : *Desnuda* Chair : 1973 : enameled iron, brass, upholstery : H 39³⁄₈" : 1983-136-1 (cat. 157)
Opposite : **185.** Javier Errando Mariscal : for Marieta Textil : *Ensaladilla* Fabric (detail) : 1978 : screen-printed cotton : W 63" : 1983-8-1 (cat 115)

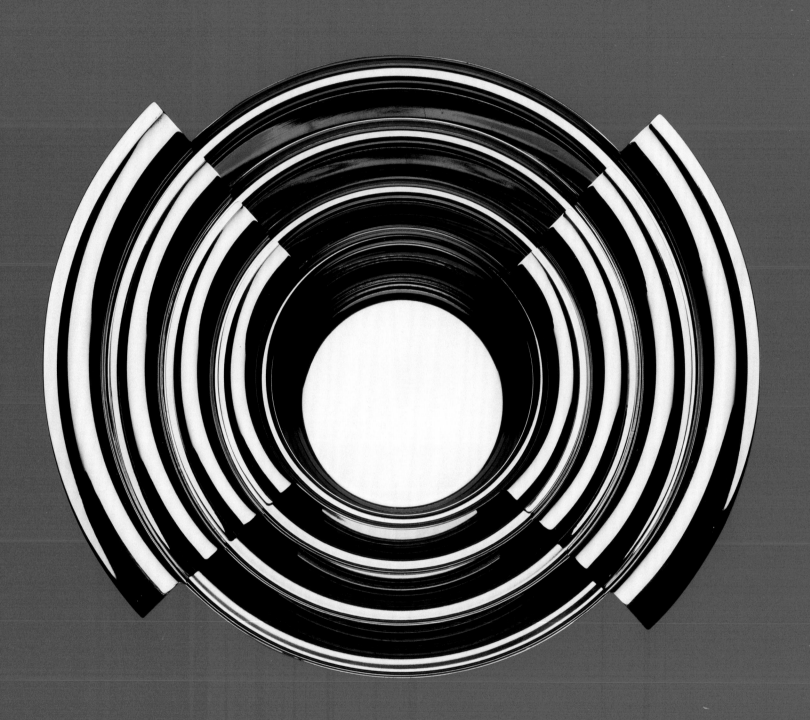

**Design Since 1945 : 1983–84**

Opposite : 186. **Roberto Sambonet** : for Sambonet : *Center Line* Cooking Set (8) : 1964 : stainless steel : D (largest pot) 9¹/₂" : 1983-141-1–8 (cat. 168)
Above : 187. **Acton Bjørn and Sigvard Bernadotte** : for Rosti : *Margrethe* Bowls (5) : 1950 : melamine : D (largest bowl) 9⁷/₁₆" : 1983-56-1–5 (cat. 20)

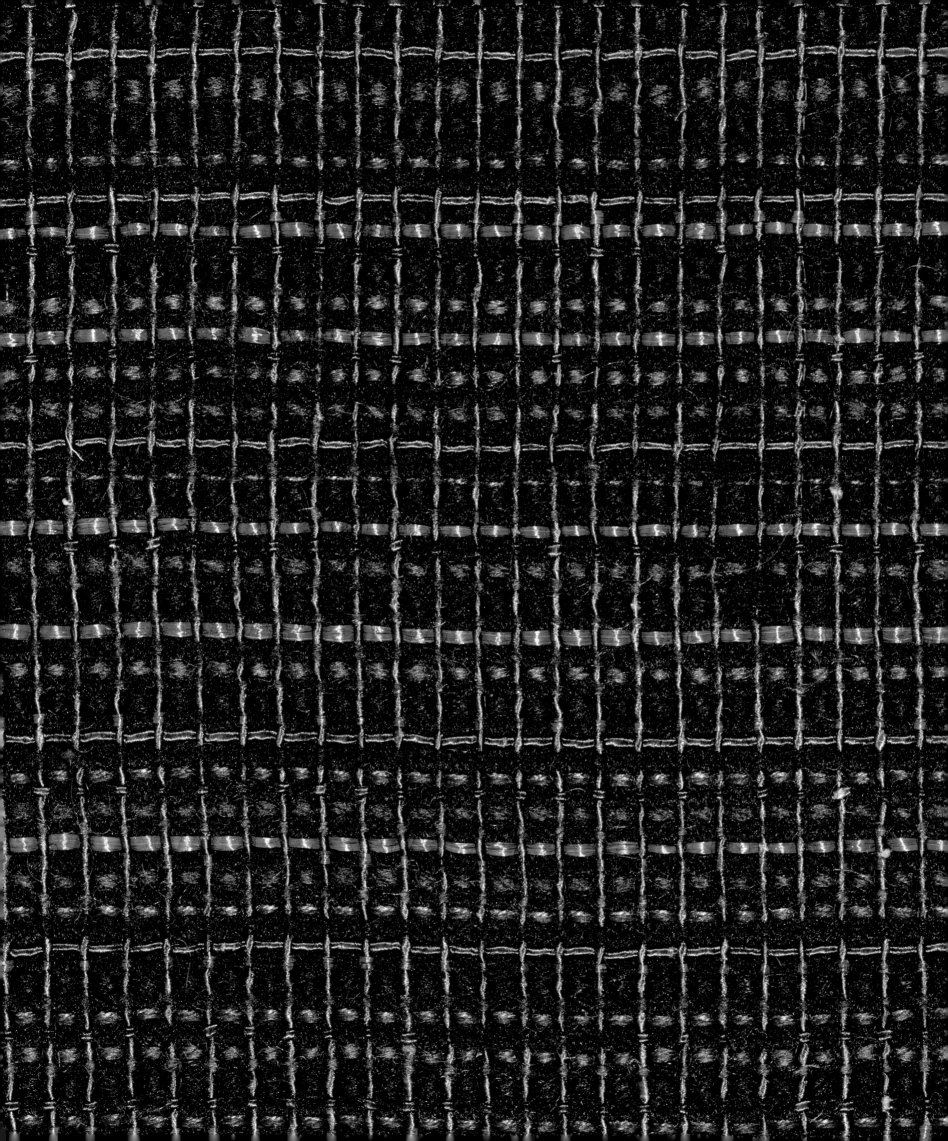

**Design Since 1945 : 1983–84**

Opposite : **193. Jack Lenor Larsen** : for Jack Lenor Larsen, Inc. : *Magnum* Fabric (detail) : 1970 : cotton, vinyl, nylon, polyamide, polyester : W 48" :
1983-186-2 (cat. 107)    Above : **194. Maija Isola** : for Marimekko Oy : *Kivet* Fabric (detail) : 1956 : screen-printed cotton : W 54" : 1983-131-3 (cat. 86)

**Design Since 1945 : 1983–84**

Opposite : 195. Daniel Weil : for Parenthesis : *Bag* Radio : 1981 : PVC plastic : H 11¹¹/₁₆" : 1983-58-1 (cat. 209)    Above : 196. Joe Colombo with Gianni Colombo : for O-Luce : *Acrilica* Table Lamp : 1962 : brass, Perspex : H 9⁷/₁₆" : 1983-134-1 (cat. 36)

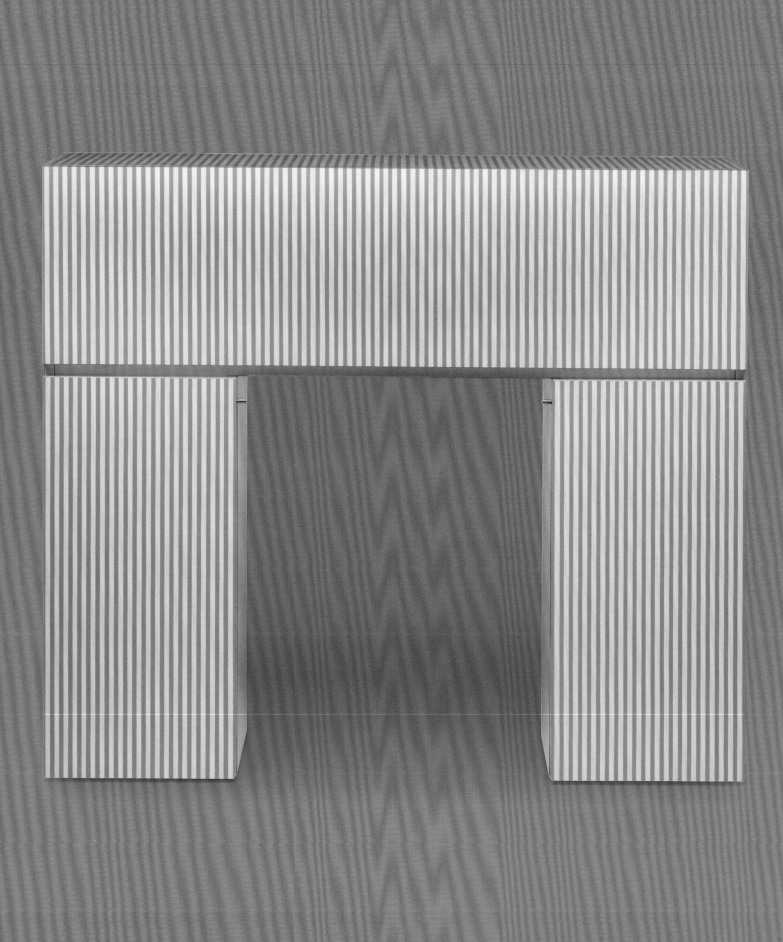

Guides to European Decorative Arts    Philadelphia Museum of Art

# Design    *1900 – 1940*

A fifth guide in the series, *Design, 1900–1940* (fig. 202), which I cowrote with my colleague George H. Marcus, head of publications at the Museum, was published in 1986 with the support of Collab. The book was celebrated in January 1987 with a reception honoring Collab and an installation of more than fifty modern and contemporary objects from the collections,[97] organized by Donna Corbin, who had joined the department to assist with *Design Since 1945*. She would take responsibility over the following years for organizing a number of thematic installations from the Museum's design collections in the Design Gallery we had maintained since 1976 as well as, on occasion, the larger Auditorium Gallery.

In 1985 I had begun organizing the major exhibition *Art Nouveau in Munich* following a year-long discussion with Hans Ottomeyer, curator of the furniture collection at the Münchner Stadtmuseum, which would provide the show with its greatest number of loans. Comprising furniture, decorative arts, textiles, graphic designs, and paintings made in Munich between 1895 and 1910, the exhibition demonstrated the importance of the city not only as a great cultural center, but also as the birthplace of a progressive new artistic style—Jugendstil—that became a foundation stone of modern design (fig. 203). The

exhibition was held in the Museum's special exhibition galleries from September to November 1988, and traveled to the Los Angeles County Museum of Art, the Saint Louis Art Museum, and the Münchner Stadtmuseum.[98] The *New York Times* headlined the show as "Innovations from Munich's Masters of Art Nouveau" and reported that "most of the material shown . . . will probably be new even to enthusiasts of the movement,"[99] while the *Philadelphia Inquirer* described it as "the kind of exhibition that museums should be willing to risk more often," exemplary for its ability to "break new ground, stimulate discussion, and further scholarship, and bring to public attention a group of objects that deserves to be seen."[100] The *Frankfurter Allgemeine Zeitung* applauded the show as a "towering occurrence" and the catalogue's "inspiring, thesis-rich" essay "as a duty to read," adding that it revealed "a supreme knowledge of the German art literature of that time."[101] The Museum purchased

**Japanese Design : A Survey Since 1950 : 1994**

Above : **211.** Exhibition catalogue : edited by Kathryn B. Hiesinger and Felice Fischer (Philadelphia: Philadelphia Museum of Art, 1994)
Opposite : **212. Hiroshi Awatsuji** : for Fujie Textile : *Jitensha* Art Screen (detail) : 1982 : screen-printed cotton : W 5' 10$^7$/$_8$":1983-118-1 (cat. 15)

The Museum received numerous gifts from manufacturers and designers in connection with *Japanese Design*, including furniture manufactured by Tendo Mokko and designed by Reiko Tanabe, Riki Watanabe (fig. 217), and Isamu Kenmochi, whose *Kashiwado* chair is built of blocks of Japanese cedar and named after a famous sumo wrestler (fig. 216). The Italian manufacturer Cappellini presented the Museum with Shiro Kuramata's *Furniture in Irregular Forms* (fig. 221). Sinya Okayama arranged for the Daichi Company to give his *Kotobuki* shelves (fig. 218), particularly because the Museum, with funds from Collab, had been the first American institution to buy the designer's *Kazenoko* stool. Sinya believes that his pieces should literally communicate with the user, and his shelves and stool suggest, in three dimensions, the forms of Japanese *kanji* pictographs, allowing the pieces to be read—*kotobuki* means "celebration," and *kazenoko* "child of the wind." Also acquired were Junichi Arai's technologically innovative fabrics (figs. 213, 215); works by Hiroshi Awatsuji (fig. 212), Kazuo Kawasaki, and Makoto Saito, most of which for the first time entered the permanent collection of a Western museum; and Issey Miyake's plastic bustier (fig. 220). Collab's support made possible the purchase of furniture by Masanori Umeda, in memory of former Collab chair Hava Gelblum (fig. 219), and by Shiro Kuramata, in honor of committee chair Gerard J. Jarosinski, Jr. (fig. 214).

**Japanese Design : A Survey Since 1950 : 1994**

Opposite : 218. Sinya Okayama : for Daichi : *Kotobuki* Shelves : 1989 : lacquered wood : H 5' 4¹/₈" : 1990-25-1 (cat. 141)    Above : 219. Masanori Umeda : for Memphis : *Ginza Robot* Cabinet : 1982 : plastic laminate, wood, chipboard : H 5' 8⁷/₈" : 1994-131-1 (cat. 195)

**Japanese Design : A Survey Since 1950 : 1994**

Above : 220. Issey Miyake : for Issey Miyake, Inc. : Bustier : 1980 : plastic : H 15" : 1992-136-1 (cat. 131)    Opposite : **221.** Shiro Kuramata :
for Cappellini : *Furniture in Irregular Forms: Side 2* Chest of Drawers : 1970 : lacquered wood : H 5' 6¹⁵/₁₆" : 1994-130-1 (cat. 102)

French words and phrases can characterize Japanese

SKILL, CARE AND WIT:
MISCELLANEOUS OBJECTS FROM JAPANESE MARKETS

THE DETAILS

THESE OBJECTS OF JAPANESE POPULAR CULTURE FASCINATE BECAUSE THEY EXHIBIT, WITH PRIDE, THESE QUALITES RARE AND PRECIOUS IN OUR TIME

**Two Naifs in Japan : Robert Venturi and Denise Scott Brown : 1994**

Opposite : **223.** Detail of objects on display   Above : **224.** Gallery view

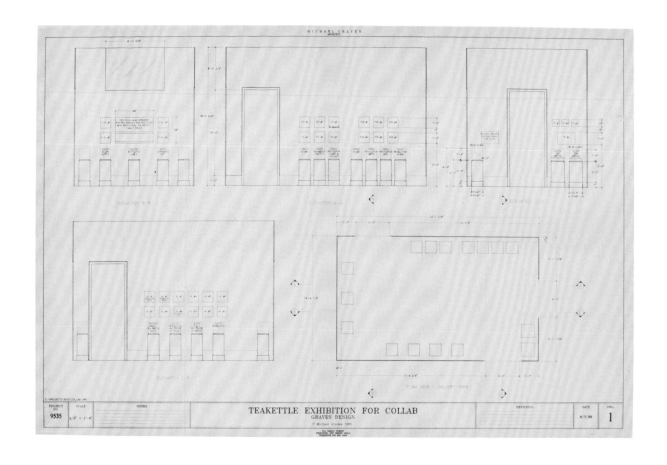

**Milton Glaser Graphic Design : Design, Influence and Process : 2000–2001**

236. Milton Glaser : for Columbia Records : *Bob Dylan* Poster : 1966 : offset lithograph : H 32⅝" : 2002-146-1 (cat. 72)

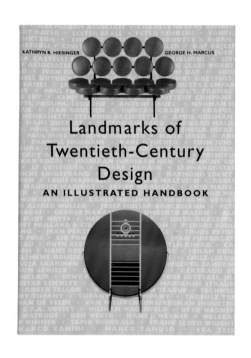  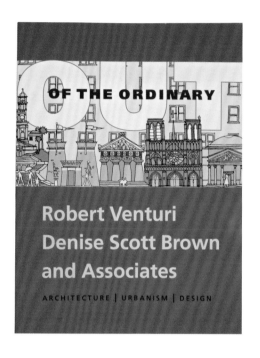

While organizing Collab's annual exhibitions, I cowrote with my colleague George Marcus two books, published by Abbeville Press, that featured objects from the Museum's design collections: *Landmarks of Twentieth-Century Design* (1993; fig. 237), widely used as a textbook, and *Antique Speak: A Guide to the Styles, Techniques, and Materials of the Decorative Arts, from the Renaissance to Art Deco* (1997; fig. 238).[123] Collaborating with architectural historians David Brownlee and David De Long, in 1997 I also began work on a major retrospective of buildings and decorative arts designed by the firm of Venturi, Scott Brown and Associates. Assisted by William Whitaker, collections manager of the University of Pennsylvania Architectural Archives, and Diane Minnite, we met regularly over many months at the Venturi archives to review the hundreds of thousands of

drawings and models that comprised the work by Venturi and his firm, from his student days to the 1990s. I also embarked on the long process of reviewing correspondence records related to the firm's decorative arts projects, my particular area of scholarly responsibility for the exhibition. *Out of the Ordinary: The Architecture and Design of Robert Venturi, Denise Scott Brown and Associates*,[124] accompanied by a catalogue of the same name and written by the organizing team (fig. 239–46), opened at the Museum in the spring of 2001—one of a series of exhibitions showcasing artists who lived or worked in Philadelphia and held in celebration of the Museum's own 125th anniversary that year. The exhibition also traveled to the Museum of Contemporary Art San Diego and to the Heinz Architectural Center at the Carnegie Museum of Art, Pittsburgh.

Above, left to right : **237.** *Landmarks of Twentieth-Century Design* : by Kathryn B. Hiesinger and George H. Marcus (New York: Abbeville, 1993)
**238.** *Antique Speak* : by Kathryn B. Hiesinger and George H. Marcus (New York: Abbeville, 1997)   **239.** *Out of the Ordinary: Robert Venturi Denise Scott Brown and Associates* : by David B. Brownlee, David G. De Long, and Kathryn B. Hiesinger (Philadelphia: Philadelphia Museum of Art, 2001)

On view were some 250 drawings, scale models, decorative art objects, photographs, and videos, with a goal of re-defining the historical position of this internationally celebrated Philadelphia firm and demonstrating the influence of its ideas and architecture over the last forty years. Designed by Tony Atkin of Atkin, Olshin, Lawson-Bell Associates, the installation also included a full-scale reproduction of the facade of the house Venturi designed for his mother, as well as his coffee-cup signboard for Grand's restaurant and a "period room" assemblage of decorative arts (figs. 240–42). The exhibition was accompanied by a lively schedule of programs, including tours, an architectural symposium, and a course on the art of architecture for schoolteachers. Reviewing the exhibition, *New Yorker* critic Paul Goldberger recognized its historical significance: "Venturi and Scott Brown's home city of

Philadelphia has never given them a major commission . . . . Philadelphia is now making up for this with 'Out of the Ordinary,' an elaborate retrospective of the firm's work. . . . It is as important in its way, as the Mies exhi-bitions, or the huge retrospective of Frank O. Gehry's work now on view at the Guggenheim."[125] The *New Republic* declared, "There is much to love in 'Out of the Ordinary.'. . . One is overwhelmed . . . by the sheer inventiveness that has poured from these architects for more than forty years."[126] *Interior Design* magazine described the cata-logue as an "authoritative and sympathetic summary of the work of one of the world's most distinguished, most adventurous, and most independent design firms."[127]

**Out of the Ordinary : The Architecture and Design of Robert Venturi, Denise Scott Brown and Associates : 2001**

240. Gallery view

**Out of the Ordinary : The Architecture and Design of Robert Venturi, Denise Scott Brown and Associates : 2001**

241 and 242. Gallery views

*Out of the Ordinary* included pieces already in the Museum's collections as well as many that would be acquired when the show closed, among them Venturi's *Sheraton* and *Chippendale* chairs for Knoll, purchased with funds provided by Collab, and his "stylized traditional" tea and coffee service for Alessi, commissioned with a "PMA" monogram by my colleague Beatrice Garvan in the Museum's American art department (fig. 246). Collab also supported the purchase of Venturi's *Notebook* and *Grandmother* printed fabrics (figs. 243, 245), made by the Fabric Workshop and Museum in Philadelphia. Marion Boulton Stroud, Museum trustee and founder of the Fabric Workshop, gave the Museum Venturi's *Gothic Revival* chair (fig. 244); the Japanese Postal Savings Promotion Society presented the chairs and table Venturi designed for the Mielmonte Hotel in Nikko, Japan; and DesignTex donated his *Gingham Floral* and other fabrics. The Museum also acquired two objects specially commissioned for a house Venturi had designed on Long Island, New York: a pair of andirons, given by Collab in honor of its chair Neil Sandvold, and a cabriole-leg table, with flat legs set alternately in front and side elevations as if they could not determine the direction in which they should be oriented. Later, when Venturi's Best Products Company showroom in Langhorne, Pennsylvania, was sold and sched-uled for renovation, the Museum received from Venturi, Scott Brown and Associates (through the new owners) a small grouping of the building's porcelain-enameled steel facade panels that had been shown in the exhibition in prototype.

**Out of the Ordinary : The Architecture and Design of Robert Venturi, Denise Scott Brown and Associates : 2001**

Opposite : **243.** Robert Venturi : for The Fabric Workshop and Museum : *Notebook* Fabric (detail) : 1982–83 : screen-printed cotton : W 57" : 1987-99-1 (cat. 201)    Above : **244.** Robert Venturi : for Knoll : *Gothic Revival* Chair : 1979–84 : laminated wood, painted plastic laminate : H 40¾" : 1999-158-1 (cat. 199)

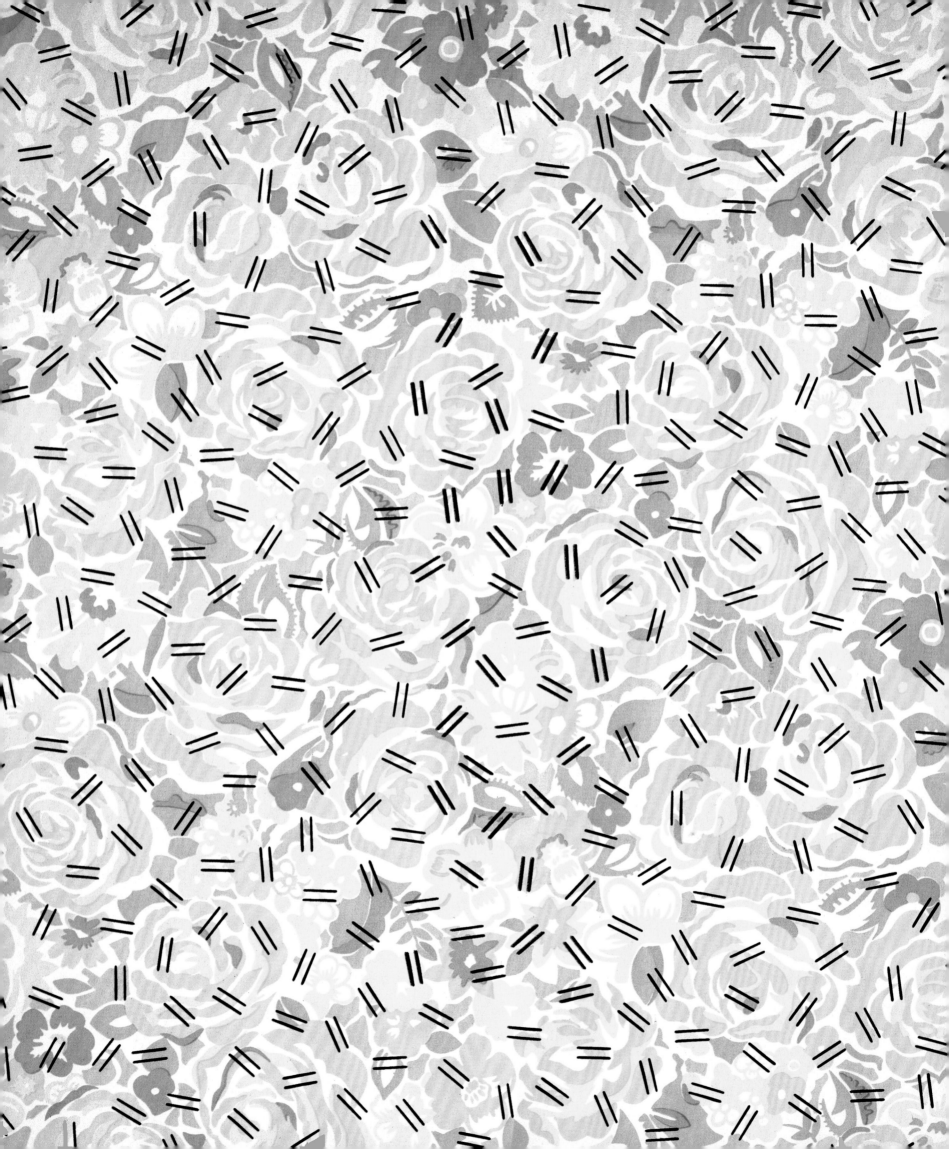

**Out of the Ordinary : The Architecture and Design of Robert Venturi, Denise Scott Brown and Associates : 2001**

Opposite : **245. Robert Venturi** : for The Fabric Workshop and Museum : *Grandmother* Fabric (detail) : 1982–83 : screen-printed cotton : W 57″ :
1987-99-2 (cat. 202)     Above: **246. Robert Venturi** : for Alessi : Tea and Coffee Service : 1980–83 : partial gilt silver : H (teapot) 10¼″ : 1986-15-1a,b–5
(cat. 200)

# THE MUSEUM'S
# 125TH ANNIVERSARY

Acenterpiece of the Museum's 125th anniversary initiatives was a campaign to acquire collection-transforming gifts of works of art, which culminated in 2002 in the exhibition *Gifts in Honor of the Museum's 125th Anniversary*.[128] Two important groups of modern furniture and decorative arts were added to the design collections and included in the exhibition. In recognition "of the strength of our modern design collection,"[129] the Museum in 1999 was offered fifteen pieces of artist-designed furniture from Lannan Foundation in Santa Fe, New Mexico. Surrealist in form and spirit, the furniture once decorated Four Winds, J. Patrick Lannan's Palm Beach estate; the gift included furniture by Diego Giacometti, Max Ernst (fig. 252), playwright Robert Wilson, and Pedro Friedeberg. Anne d'Harnoncourt wrote me. "I'm *thrilled* about the Giacomettis . . . and the Ernst bed sounds *wild—def.* worth going to see (*only* cautious given obvious size question). And if you go look maybe they have *even* more stuff?"[130]

The second group of furniture and objects acquired had been assembled by collectors of Joe Colombo's work,[131] who additionally arranged for Mr. and Mrs. Benjamin Thompson's gift of the designer's *Mini-Kitchen* on casters (fig. 249).[131] Collab funded the purchase of the Colombo collection as its 125th Anniversary gift to the Museum. The acquisition included a wide variety of Colombo's designs, including furniture, lighting, glassware, and his *Linea 72* in-flight service for Alitalia, with both first-class and disposable economy-class utensils (figs. 247, 248, 250, 251). All of these objects were designed to function in a variety of ways, underlining Colombo's deep-seated conviction that objects and their users interact in constantly changing patterns of relationship.

Planning the actual celebration of the Museum's anniversary had been a subject of much internal discussion beginning in the winter of 1998–99. With the support of Anne d'Harnoncourt and Gail Harrity, I proposed that the building itself should be the subject of our plans, and invited New York architects Elizabeth Diller and Ricardo Scofidio to design an installation project featuring the Museum.

**Gifts in Honor of the Museum's 125th Anniversary : 2002**

Opposite : **247. Joe Colombo** : for Kartell : Armchair : 1964 : painted plywood : H 22³/₄" : 2001-42-2 (cat. 32)     Above : **248. Joe Colombo** : for Kartell : *Vademecum* Folding Lamp : 1986 : ABS plastic, stainless steel : H 9⁷/₈" : 2001-42-4 (cat. 33)

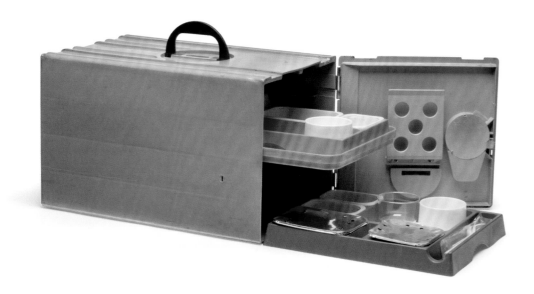

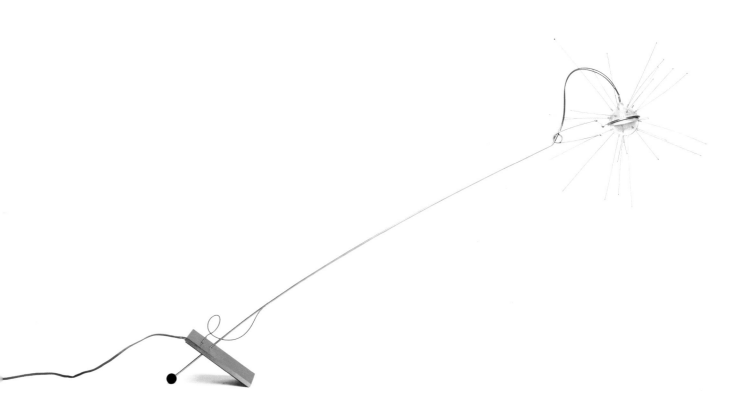

spring lecture series and a newsletter in an effort to build and inform Collab's audience. A regular feature of the publication has been a description of the Museum's recent acquisitions along with a "wish list" of desiderata, often happily marked "Donated—Thank You!"

Although few Collab members at the time knew the work of German lighting designer Ingo Maurer when I proposed his name in 2002, the committee supported not only his award for design excellence (fig. 201) but also the challenges of two separate Museum installations in dramatically different galleries, collectively referred to as *The Light Magic of Ingo Maurer*.[137] Over the years Maurer had generously donated his *YaYaHo* lighting system and *Bibibi*, *Mozzkito*, and *Kokoro* lamps to the Museum (figs. 258, 259). For one section of Collab 2002, I asked him to relight our eighteenth-century French period room from the Château of Draveil. Maurer hung his *Porca Miseria!* chandelier—a light sculpture made of broken porcelain dishes—from the central ceiling rosette and surrounded it with walls of wire mesh (fig. 257). The reflections were endlessly repeated in the room's large mirror glasses, leading Maurer to remark that "a room within a room is a room, is a room," in a playful allusion to poet Gertrude Stein.[138] As the second

part of Collab 2002, Maurer installed in the design gallery his *aha SoSo* lighting system over a floor piece painted in DayGlo orange, white, and gray.[139] Maurer's dazzling installations were heralded by the *Philadelphia Inquirer* and illustrated in the *New York Times Magazine*.[140] In recognition of his recent pleated-paper lamps such as *Kokoro*, the student competition asked participants to design a table lamp made primarily of paper, a popular project that attracted over two hundred entries. In honor of Collab chair James Fulton, the committee gave the Museum Maurer's *Wo bist du, Edison?* lamp, which features a hologram of a lightbulb with a socket shaped like the silhouetted profile of Thomas Edison.

**The Light Magic of Ingo Maurer : 2002–3**

Opposite : 257. Ingo Maurer's installation of *Porca Miseria!* in the Museum's eighteenth-century French period room from the Château of Draveil : 2002
Above : 258. **Ingo Maurer** : for Ingo Maurer GmbH : *Mozzkito* Lamp : 1996 : metal, plastic, rubber : L 31½" : 1999-12-1 (cat. 121)
Below : 259. **Ingo Maurer and Dagmar Mombach** : for Ingo Maurer GmbH : *Kokoro* Lamp : 1998 : pleated paper, metal : H 30" : 2002-218-1 (cat. 122)

251

260. David Tisdale : for David Tisdale Design : *Picnic* Flatware : 1985 : anodized aluminum : L (knife) 8" : 2003-14-1–3 (cat. 194)

# PLANS FOR EXPANSION

Collab 2003 celebrated the Museum's public announcement of the previous year that Gluckman Mayner Architects of New York would design the renovation of and addition to the former Fidelity Building (to be renamed the Ruth and Raymond G. Perelman Building in honor of its principal donors), which would house the Collab Gallery. Ahead of the groundbreaking celebration, which took place in 2004, the exhibition *Work in Progress: Gluckman Mayner Designs the Perelman Building*[141] illustrated the process of architectural planning and design through drawings, photographs, models, and samples of materials. The *Philadelphia Inquirer* applauded the exhibition's efforts to "demystify the profession" and demonstrate that "good architecture is as much about solving problems as it is about creating eye-popping sculpture."[142] In conjunction with the show, Richard Gluckman spoke about his work, while students in Collab's annual competition were asked to design the main exterior signage for the Perelman Building as it might appear after the renovation. The year 2003 also saw the decorative arts department collaborate with Philadelphia's Fabric Workshop and Museum for the exhibition *On the Wall: Wallpaper and Tableau*.[143] Diane Minnite coordinated the Museum's loans of historic papers, for which it received in exchange—as gifts of trustee Marion Boulton Stroud, the artists, and an anonymous donor—a group of contemporary wallpapers, ranging from Virgil Marti's *Bullies* in fluorescent ink and rayon flock on Tyvek to Francesco Simeti's *Arabian Nights* notations on the war in Afghanistan to Andy Warhol's *Cows*. Also in 2003, Donna Corbin organized an exhibition of twentieth-century flatware. *Have a Bite: 20th-Century Flatware from the Collection*,[144] included eleven newly acquired flatware services, among them David Tisdale's anodized aluminum *Picnic* set (fig. 260) and Michael Schneider's *Mono Tools* flatware, the latter inspired by prehistoric archaeology.

In 2004 we were able to coax eighty-seven-year-old Florence Knoll Bassett out of retirement to design and curate for Collab 2005 the first solo museum exhibition of her legendary work. *Florence Knoll Bassett: Defining Modern*,[145] which I organized, had repercussions far beyond its size. Publicity was extensive and international, appearing in the *New York Times* and *Philadelphia Inquirer* as well as the magazines *Architecture, House and Garden, Metropolis, Casamica* in Italy, and *SDQ Magazine* in Australia. Bassett had led an entirely private life since leaving Knoll, Inc., in 1965, but she had lost none of her considerable design skills or desire for perfection. She sent the Museum her model of the gallery as

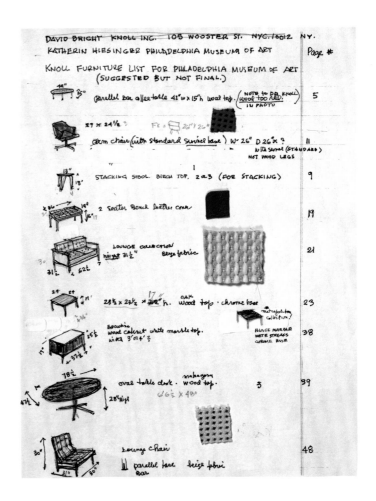

**Florence Knoll Bassett : Defining Modern : 2004–5**

261. Florence Knoll Bassett's exhibition list : 2004

**Florence Knoll Bassett : Defining Modern : 2004–5**

Above : 262. Florence Knoll : for Knoll : Credenza : 1955 : chromed steel, mahogany, marble : L 37" : 2005-20-1 (cat. 100)   Opposite : 263. Gallery view

it should be installed and a hand-drawn illustrated exhibition list, complete with samples of fabric and veneer (fig. 261), following a presentation strategy she had begun while a student at the Architectural Association in London and had developed when the Planning Unit was formed at Knoll. Under the direction of David Bright, Knoll's vice-president of communications, the company produced furniture for the show to Bassett's specifications, while the Museum's installation design department, under the able direction of Jack Schlechter, helped realize her plans, resulting in one of the most perfect uses of the space to date (fig. 263). In conjunction with the exhibition, the Museum published an illustrated chronology of Florence Knoll's career and furniture designs, distributed as a gallery hand-out and funded by a generous grant from Elise Jaffe

and Jeffrey Brown of New York. At the opening of the exhibition Bassett was presented with Collab's Design Excellence Award in absentia, and I delivered a lecture about her work that I had developed in close communication with the designer herself. Carl Magnusson, Knoll's design director, also spoke about Bassett's influence on the company she had cofounded. Collab's Student Design Competition asked for redesigns of a piece of Knoll's classic furniture, using new materials and new production technologies. A chair and table as well as a credenza designed by Bassett were made by the firm for the exhibition; the chair and table were donated to the Museum by Knoll, Inc., and the credenza by Collab to honor committee chair Robert Aibel (fig. 262).

The Museum's design gallery was transformed again by Collab 2005, *Gaetano Pesce: Pushing the Limits*.[146] Few Italian designers have taken material and technological experimentation further than Pesce, who most recently has produced furniture and objects that vary in color and shape according to the chance flow of pigmented plastic resin in molds. For the opening of the exhibition, he designed a unique invitation in flexible resin. The show included a self-portrait with miniature chairs outlining Pesce's silhouette, an architectural model, chairs, lamps, and carpet prototypes. A number of the chairs were recent acquisitions by gift and purchase, among them, the *I Feltri* armchair (fig. 267) in low- and high-backed versions made of thick wool felt—soaked in resin at the bottom for support and flexible at the top so that the user can manipulate the shape—along with two chairs and a table from Pesce's *Nobody's Perfect* series (fig. 266). Several bracelets, also in flexible resin, were added to the collections after the exhibition (figs. 264, 265). The accompanying Student Design Competition was based on Pesce's use of nonstandard production processes, and asked for a full-scale functional prototype of a flower vase that reflected the designer's approach to variable production. Entries included a container molded out of soil and wax and others fashioned from pipe fittings, recycled concrete, and tree roots; first prize was awarded to a vase made of ice with flowers frozen into its surface. The "wildly varied" exhibition of the "always provocative" designer received front-page coverage in the "Home and Design" section of the *Philadelphia Inquirer*.[147]

**Gaetano Pesce : Pushing the Limits : 2005–6**

Above, clockwise from top : **264. Gaetano Pesce** : for Fish Design : *Spaghetti* Bracelet : 2005 : plastic resin : D 4 1/2" : 2005-183-1 (cat. 148)
**265. Gaetano Pesce** : for Fish Design : *Ribbon* Bracelet : 2005 : plastic resin : D 4" : 2005-102-2 (cat. 149)   **266. Gaetano Pesce** : for Zerodisegno :
*Nobody's Perfect* Chair : 2002 : polyurethane-based resin, nylon : H (seat) 17 11/16" : 2003-136-1 (cat. 147)   Opposite : **267. Gaetano Pesce** : for Cassina :
*I Feltri* Armchair (Lowback) : 1986 : wool felt with polyester resin, felt, cotton, hemp string, fabric : H 38 5/8" : 2006-32-1 (cat. 146)

electrostatic coating applied to the interior, allowing bread to be kept warm long after it is moved from the oven to the table.

*Georg Jensen Silversmiths* was the last exhibition to be mounted by the department in the design gallery located in the heart of the Museum's modern and contemporary painting and sculpture collections. Design objects had occupied the gallery since 1976, but in anticipation of the opening of the Collab Gallery in the new building the small, 330-square-foot room reverted to painting and sculpture, d'Harnoncourt arguing the need for space as well as her conviction that the changing design exhibitions held there interrupted the overall Museum aesthetic. The decision left modern and contemporary painting and sculpture the only section of the Museum where works of art in all mediums are not exhibited together, as Fiske Kimball had conceived. James Nelson Kise, trustee and from 2001 to 2009 chair of the departmental advisory committee,[149] nevertheless advocated continuing Kimball's historical progression of decorative arts on Fairmount into the present.[150] Having given the Museum its first Olivetti typewriter—the classic *Lettera 22*, designed by Marcello Nizzoli (fig. 270)—Kise has continuously supported the Museum's acquisition and exhibition of modern and contemporary objects, particularly since 1994 when, with the promise that "it might be more fun"[151] than his previous trustee assignments, he joined the departmental committee. Nevertheless, as of this writing, modern and contemporary design (with the exception of contemporary American craft) continues to lack gallery space in the main Museum building.

In 2006 Collab gave its award for design excellence to the Danish silverware firm of Georg Jensen, bringing a different audience to the Museum and the exhibition that accompanied the award. With an installation design by Jack Schlechter, *Georg Jensen Silversmiths*[148] comprised over 120 objects from the Museum's permanent collection, the collections of Georg Jensen AS in Copenhagen, and private collections in Britain and the United States (figs. 268, 269) The exhibition was an exercise in installing a great many objects in a very small space without sacrificing aesthetic appeal or intelligibility. Grouped by designer, the silver was displayed along with facsimiles of the original design drawings for many of the pieces. Featured was the work of Georg Jensen, who founded the eponymous firm in 1904, Sigvard Bernadotte, Piet Hein, Søren Georg Jensen, Henning Koppel, Harald Nielsen, Verner Panton, Johan Rohde, Allan Scharff, and Magnus Stephensen. Hans-Kristian Højsgaard, president and chief executive officer of the Jensen firm, accepted Collab's Design Excellence Award on behalf of the company. Based on Georg Jensen's use of ornament, the student competition invited designs of an "intelligent ornament" that reflected the vernacular of the firm's founder and its enduring values. The winning project was a leafy, openwork breadbasket with an

**Georg Jensen Silversmiths : 2006–7**

Top : 268. Gallery view    Bottom : 269. Søren Georg Jensen : for Georg Jensen Sølvsmedie : Condiment Set for Salt, Pepper, and Mustard, *no. 965* : 1951 : silver : H (pepper shaker) 3 1/8" : 1982-58-4a–c (cat. 94)

**Designing Modern : 2007–8**

278. Gaetano Pesce : for B & B Italia : *Up 5* Chair and *Up 6* Ottoman : 1969 : polyurethane foam, stretch jersey : H (chair) 40¹/₂" :
D (ottoman) 22¹/₂" : 2000-151-1,2 (cat. 145)

David Mayner. Afterward, Lisa Roberts wrote: "I'm just blown away. The building, the gallery, and the exhibit have all done our gift justice. . . . Your contribution, building modern and contemporary design at the [Museum] into a significant collection, will now have the opportunity to be seen, to be 'heard' and to make a difference. . . . Here's to our future together!"[157]

In conjunction with the opening of the Collab Gallery and the exhibition, information mapping was the theme of the Student Design Competition, which asked participants to map the history of modern design in the twentieth and twenty-first centuries. The winning project illustrated the development of modern chairs according to their formal characteristics.

Top : **280. Jacques-Émile Ruhlmann** : Chair : 1924 : rosewood, fabric upholstery : H 31⁷/₈" : 2006-77-1 (cat.164)    **Jacques-Émile Ruhlmann** : Writing Desk : c. 1925 : Macassar ebony, ivory, suede : H 44¹/₂" : 1976-227-1 (cat. 165)    Bottom : **281.** Left to right: Lisa Roberts, Anne d'Harnoncourt, David Seltzer, and Lisa Benn at Collab 2007

**Visual Delight : Ornament and Pattern in Modern and Contemporary Design : 2009**

Opposite : **296. Patricia Urquiola** : for Moroso : *Antibodi* Chaise : 2006 : stainless steel, PVC plastic, polyurethane, felt : L 5' 1 13/16" : 2008-57-1
(cat. 196)  Above : **297–300. Elizabeth Garouste and Mattia Bonetti** : for Porzellanmanufaktur Reichenbach and Anthologie Quartett : Plates from
*Étrange Végetation* : 1992 : porcelain : D (large dinner plate, bottom) 11 13/16" : 2004-141-2,3,4,9 (cat. 64–67)

**Visual Delight : Ornament and Pattern in Modern and Contemporary Design : 2009**

**301. Tord Boontje** : for Artecnica : *Midsummer* Light : 2004 : Tyvek : H 30" : 2008-178-3 (cat. 22)

**Richard Schultz : Five Decades of Design : 2009**

Top : 302. Richard Schultz at the exhibition    Bottom, left and right : 303. **Richard Schultz** : for Richard Schultz Design : *Topiary* Lounge Chair and
Ottoman : 1988 : aluminum with epoxy polyester powder coating : H (chair) 30¹/2" : H (ottoman) 15" : 2006-119-1,2 (cat. 175)

In June 2009, while modern and contemporary design was enjoying unprecedented visibility in these three simultaneous exhibitions, the Museum's board of trustees announced the election of Timothy Rub, at the time director of the Cleveland Museum of Art, as the institution's thirteenth director, succeeding the late Anne d'Harnoncourt.[170] Like Edwin Atlee Barber and Fiske Kimball generations earlier, Rub brought to the directorship a record of work, publications, and interest in the fields of decorative arts and architecture, with a particular taste for modernism. Trained at Middlebury College (B.A.) and New York University (M.A.), he served as curator at the Cooper-Hewitt Museum from 1983 to 1987, where he organized the exhibition *Vienna/New York: The Work of Joseph Urban*—described by the *New York Times* as "comprehensive . . . and unusually rich in the objects it contains."[171]

To the delight of Philadelphia's architecture and design community, the Museum's new director led a standing ovation for Dutch designer Marcel Wanders, the recipient of the Design Excellence Award at Collab 2009 (fig. 305), and at the reception afterward participated enthusiastically in the performance piece *Happy Hour Chandelier*, designed and conceived by Nanette Linning and Wanders (fig. 304).

**Marcel Wanders : Daydreams : 2009–10**

Above and opposite, left to right : **304.** *Happy Hour Chandelier* : 2009 : a performance piece conceived and designed by Nanette Linning and Marcel Wanders      **305.** Timothy Rub (right), named Museum director in 2009, with Neil Sandvold (left) and Marcel Wanders (center) at the exhibition opening  **306.** Gallery view

*Marcel Wanders: Daydreams* was the designer's first solo exhibition in the United States, for which he selected his favorite works of the last two decades and around them designed a unique multimedia installation in the Collab Gallery (fig. 306).[172] The shifting video images, light, and sound were choreographed with the Museum's first "show controller"—technology that can simultaneously operate multiple electronic devices—managed by the Museum's team of Stephen A. Keever, Jennifer Schlegel, and James J. Fraatz and resulting in the most complex audiovisual project in the institution's history. The exhibition's dazzling results were acclaimed to be "as surreal, exaggerated,

and playful as its name suggests," according to the *Philadelphia Inquirer*.[173] Gifts to the design collections from the show came from several manufacturers, including Bisazza, Cappellini, Flos, and Wanders himself. At the final board of trustees meeting of 2009, Rub noted that he hoped the Museum would acquire Wanders's *Wallflower* light sculpture (as it did in 2010; fig. 307), a group of fifty-two color-changing LEDs dispersed through glass flowers—a wall-mounted circular bouquet that is intended to be programmed as a calendar, its color changes paced to celebrate different occasions.[174]

And so this history ends as it began, with the quest for acquisitions of contemporary decorative arts for the Museum. Collab marked its fortieth anniversary in 2010. It is safe to say that, powered by the group's advocacy and support of the last four decades, the Philadelphia Museum of Art can now lay claim to one of the most important modern and contemporary design collections to be found in any comprehensive museum. Supported by the Museum's directors and executive officers over many years, the program of design exhibitions large and small has driven the rapid growth of the collections, thanks to the generosity of manufacturers, designers, and many private individuals. This is a story with a happy ending in the present and the promise of a very bright future

**Marcel Wanders : Daydreams : 2009–10**

307. Marcel Wanders : for Flos : *Wallflower* Light Sculpture : 2009 : glass, aluminum, electronic components : D (overall) 55 1/8" : 2010-101-1 (cat. 205)

# INDEX

# PHOTOGRAPHY CREDITS

Objects in the collection of the Philadelphia Museum of Art were photographed by Graydon Wood, Lynn Rosenthal, Andrea Nuñez, and Jason Wierzbicki except as noted.

Alessi S.p.A., Crusinallo, Italy: p. 9

*Annual Report, Pennsylvania Museum and School of Industrial Art* (Philadelphia, 1878): fig. 15; (Philadelphia, 1903): fig. 27; (Philadelphia, 1911): fig. 54; (Philadelphia, 1916): fig. 60

*Bulletin of the Pennsylvania Museum*, vol. 3, no. 10 (April 1, 1905): fig. 29; vol. 15, no. 57 (January 1917): fig. 30; vol. 18, no. 76 (April 1923): fig. 62; vol. 21, no. 99 (January 1926): fig. 53; vol. 22, no. 107 (November 1926): fig. 67; vol. 23, no. 117 (December 1927–January 1928): fig. 69; vol. 26, no. 142 (May 1931): fig. 77; vol. 30, no. 165 (January 1935): fig. 87

*Bulletin of the Philadelphia Museum of Art*, vol. 49, no. 242 (Summer 1954): fig. 118; vol. 60, nos. 283/84 (October 1, 1964): fig. 130; vol. 61, nos. 287/88 (October 1, 1965): fig. 74; vol. 65, no. 304 (July–September 1970): fig. 138

John Condax: figs. 116, 160

Sigurd Fischer: fig. 71

Flos S.p.A., Brescia, Italy: pp. 2–3.

Free Library of Philadelphia, Print and Picture Collection: figs. 6, 14

Mark Garvin: fig. 271

John Getting, courtesy of Maharam: back endpapers

Andrew Harkins: fig. 65

Kelly & Massa: figs. 201, 281, 303

Andrea Nuñez: fig. 295

Philadelphia Museum of Art, Archives, Decorative Arts Department Records: figs. 253–56; Founding Documents Collection: figs. 16–19; Records of the Directors, Exhibition Records: fig. 137; Special Format, Architectural Drawings: fig. 86

Philadelphia Museum of Art, Library: figs. 1, 2

Matt Wargo, courtesy of John Izenour, Venturi, Scott Brown and Associates: figs. 223, 224

Stuart Watson Photography: p. 303

James Jason Wierzbicki: figs. 284, 302

# ABOUT THE AUTHOR

Kathryn Bloom Hiesinger is curator of European Decorative Arts after 1700 at the Philadelphia Museum of Art, a position she has held since 1972, and has also taught and lectured widely. She was educated at Wellesley College and Harvard University, where she received her A.M. and Ph.D. in the history of art. Her interests and publications have ranged from sixteenth-century Italian tomb monuments to the decorative arts of the French eighteenth century and Second Empire to contemporary design. She is the recipient of numerous honors and awards including France's Chevalier of the Order of Arts and Letters.

Russel Wright : for Iroquois China : Covered Casserole from *Iroquois Casual China* Service : 1946 : glazed porcelain : H 5 1/4" : 1983-45-1 (cat. 219) :
The author dined on Wright's *Iroquois Casual China* at her family's home; the casserole was a gift of her parents, Mr. and Mrs. Benjamin Bloom, in 1983.

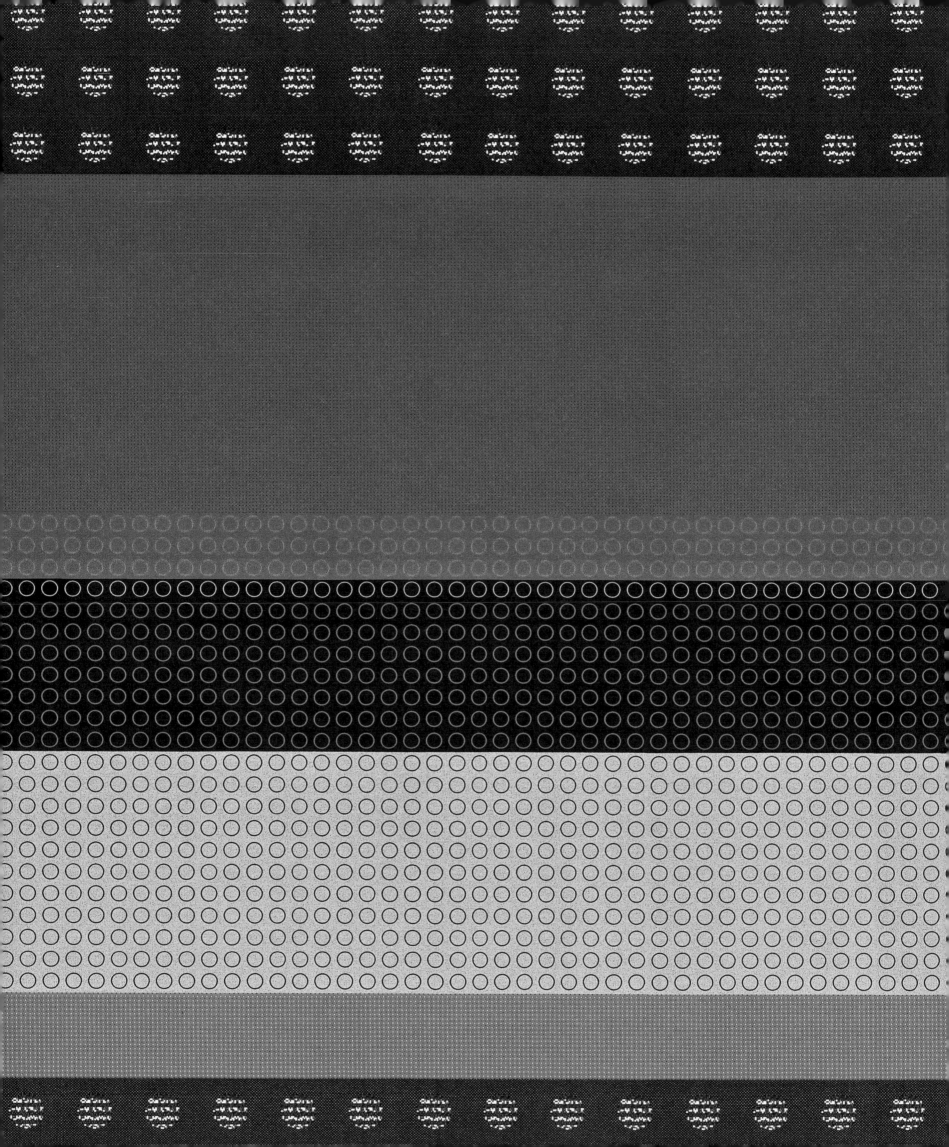